TIME OUT OF MIND

Going Places (1969)

I Would Have Saved Them If I Could (1975)

The Men's Club (1981)

Shuffle (1990)

To Feel These Things (1993)

Sylvia (1992)

TIME
OUT OF MIND

THE DIARIES OF
LEONARD MICHAELS
1961–1995

RIVERHEAD BOOKS

A MEMBER OF PENGUIN PUTNAM INC.

NEW YORK

1999

RIVERHEAD BOOKS
a member of
Penguin Putnam Inc.
375 Hudson Street
New York, NY 10014

Library of Congress Cataloging-in-Publication Data

Michaels, Leonard, date.
Time out of mind : the diaries of Leonard Michaels, 1961–1995 /
Leonard Michaels.
p. cm.
ISBN 1-57322-142-2 (acid-free paper)
1. Michaels, Leonard, date.—Diaries.
2. Authors, American—20th century—Diaries.
I. Title.
PS3563.I273 Z47   1999   99-19020 CIP
818'.5403—dc21
[B]

Printed in the United States of America

1   3   5   7   9   10   8   6   4   2

This book is printed on acid-free paper. ♾

Book design by Claire Naylon Vaccaro

TO KATHARINE

TIME OUT OF MIND

I began to keep a journal in 1961, when I lived with my girlfriend in a tenement on MacDougal Street in Greenwich Village. The walls were thin and the neighbors heard much of what we said to each other, because it was often said at the top of our lungs. We fought almost daily. Despite what the neighbors heard, I considered it dishonorable to talk to anyone—even old friends or family—about personal troubles. So I talked to nobody and kept a secret journal. When Iago says there are men "so loose of soul" they talk even in their sleep, he doesn't mean me.

By the time my girlfriend and I got married, I was going to my journal as if to prayer, and I began putting down whatever came to mind—incidents, reflections, gossip, etc., not just troubles. I said many things I wouldn't say to anyone but myself. Not because they were scandalous or shameful, but because they were of peculiar interest only to me. I wondered if my journal were a form of self-indulgence, a too private luxury, but I continued to write in it long after my wife died. I married again, then again ten years later. I had two boys with the second wife, a girl with the third, and my journal accumulated in dozens of notebooks. I took them wherever I went in America and Europe, a heavy package bound with twine. I lugged it through airports and the streets of foreign cities. In hotel rooms and rented apartments, I looked for hiding places. I never left the notebooks in my car, and even carried the pile into restaurants in Paris and Rome and shoved it under my chair. I'd heard about thieves who, breaking into cars to steal lug-

gage, also took the irreplaceable manuscript of a novel or a book of poems or a doctoral dissertation.

I never read my notebooks. I just carried them everywhere, like a child with a favorite blanket. I didn't want them to get stolen or lost, but mainly I didn't want anyone else to read them. I'd written a good deal in a rush of feeling, sometimes in distress and confusion. I believed the notebooks contained "real feelings," not social feelings. The most banal entry—a description of a dinner party or a telephone call—suggested that something in the moment had engaged me, was actually felt. I couldn't say exactly what was felt while I wrote it, but the mystery gave value to my journals. I wrote somewhat the way people take photos, for contemplation later, though I had no idea when later would be and I didn't relish the prospect. Recognizing yourself in journal entries, as in old photos, is not a simple pleasure. You might feel a desire to redo your life, and be wiser and better, or much worse.

About thirty years after my first wife died, I decided to write a memoir of the marriage. I consulted the notebooks where I'd recorded her comments about me, and then decided to quote her comments, letting her speak for herself. In this way she lived in her uniquely wonderful manner and the silence of my journal was compromised. Years later, when an editor at The New Yorker asked if he might look at some of my journal entries for publication, I couldn't think why not. I'd already published exceedingly personal entries. Besides, times had changed and so had my perspective. The contents of my journal no longer seemed taboo. I selected a number of entries that, a little while earlier, I'd not have wanted anyone to read, and they were published.

Occasionally when writing about an incident it became a story, or while describing the gesture of some friend it grew into a character only vaguely like the friend, as if sentence rhythms and the myriad relations of words had a life of their own, and, like a dream, language speaks us more than we know. At a deeper level of consideration, it must seem that everyone except children is susceptible to the beauties and corruptions of form, and not merely in storytelling. Plato thought this susceptibility was the erotic highway to truth. *Mathematicians talk about the allure of formal beauty or elegant proofs. When revising a sentence for the sake of a more pleasing sound, I sometimes found—suddenly—that it made better sense. This seems to me inexplicable, but then how we say anything at all, let alone write it, isn't easy to explain.*

For Time out of Mind, *there are many new selections from my journals. A number of them have been edited for clarity, though nothing is very polished or defended. Names of the dead and famous are real, and so are most other names. When it seemed necessary, I asked for permission to quote. Nobody refused. When people asked to read what I said about them, I deleted the passages.*

I've disguised a few people who might otherwise be embarrassed or arrested. If I had invented all the people, I would have called this book a novel, but they invented themselves and belong only to life and journalism, not literary imagination. As would be true of anybody's journal, an autobiographical story, like an underground stream, surfaces here and there, from years ago to now.

Jan. 21, '61
Sylvia's girlfriends are Naomi, Susie, Sally, Jolie, Ellen, and Baiba. Boyfriends are Harvey and Steve. All can be categorized by a few major facts—pretty, handsome, smart, wealthy, good, bad, depressed, funny. If you're one thing you can't be two or three, at least not fully. If someone is good, almost everything else seems trivial.

Jan. 27, '61
Ernie calls from Chicago. He says there is a conspiracy of politicians and "the mob" to make the price of a certain stock shoot up. "The mayor is in on it," he says, and insists that I raise money however I can—get it from friends or family—and buy as much of the stock as possible. I've already forgotten the name of the stock. In a few days he will call again and tell me to sell. Then the stock will crash. He sounds like a movie gangster, talking out of the side of his mouth not to be overheard. He was concerned to have me benefit from the conspiracy. I was touched, and I wished I could oblige him and get rich, but I don't have any money to invest in stocks, crooked or otherwise. Why is Ernie concerned to involve me? Is he fond of me? We haven't talked for over a year, not since we were roommates in Ann Arbor. He has a big soft white face with large brown eyes. Looks sensuous and womanly. Maybe he just wanted to talk to me and felt he needed a reason. You can always talk to a person about

how to become rich. Ernie talks only about money, food, possessions. He becomes interested in someone if he thinks the person is useful, either as a means of getting rich or having sex. I'm neither. He phones anyway, so he probably misses me. Ernie has no job. He schemes constantly and will do anything not to work. Except when I was a little kid, I've always worked.

Feb. 5, '61

A piece of Danish pastry lies where Sylvia left it on wax paper on the middle shelf of the refrigerator. It's been there for days. Now and then she chips off a bit—shedding crumbs and flakes of icing—and eats it. She won't eat it all at once. That would be too fattening. She's five foot six, weighs one hundred and fifteen pounds, and looks slender. Her inner thighs, soft and doughy, were once heavier. I wanted to toss the piece of Danish into the garbage, but I'm curious to see how long she will leave it in the refrigerator and pick at it. The sticky wax paper gathers miscellaneous droppings from higher shelves and tiny roaches have penetrated the refrigerator seal.

A spooky-looking gray female cat lives with us. Cat, fleas, roaches, mice, and us in a room and a half. The toilet is down the hall; a narrow closet, an overhead tank and long chain. Forty bucks a month plus utilities. There are regular people in the building, local Italians with their kids. There are also artists—actors, writers, painters. Only Darden, the actor who lives upstairs, has reputation. A startlingly beautiful dark-haired girl appeared at our door, looking for Darden. I told her he lived upstairs. She said thanks and left. I was upset. If she hadn't knocked at our door, I'd not have suddenly thought this building is old and grim and smelly.

Feb. 6, '61

I was hired at a teacher's college, Paterson State, and went to my first faculty meeting. Several colleagues spoke with considerable excitement about some girl—a student—who has embarrassed them and others. They didn't say how, only that she ought to be thrown out of school and she would be if her average weren't one tenth of a point higher than the flunking average which is required by state regulation for expulsion. One said that she shouldn't ever be permitted to teach, and Fern, red-faced and blowsy, shrieked, "That girl will drag the name of Paterson State College through the mud." I wanted to ask who she is, but didn't dare lest they imagine things. The idea of her dragging us through the mud was interesting, better than talk about teaching methods.

The students chat during class. I lost my temper and said, "You don't have to be here. Leave right now if you want to." I was shaking with anger. None of them left. A student came up afterward and told me chatting was common in class. I had to tell them off, or put up with it. I told Chairman McCrae. He offered to tell the president and have the students pulled out of the class. Tell the president? I felt like a fool for having lost my temper.

Feb. 9, '61
The water to the building was cut off. Some problem with pipes. I went up to the roof, collected snow in a pan, then put it on the stove and lighted the burner to heat the snow and make water for coffee. The snow melted, turning into gray water and black bits of filth. I was surprised. Beautiful white snow falling on the rooftops is mainly filth.

Feb. 10, '61
Ernie calls and asks if I have invested. I said, "I don't have any money." He says the stock has gone way up in value. "It made history." I said again I don't have any money. He said he can tell me

how to get money from a bank without collateral. Another scheme. "Do what I'm telling you. It's not too late, but it will be soon." I asked if he has made a lot of money. He said he has made a fortune on paper. He was holding the stock for a few more days. It would continue to go up in value. Then it would crash. He would sell shortly before that happens. He was laughing in little gasps, a sort of weak cackling, and practically begging me to invest. Why does my involvement mean so much to him? He's like the pot smokers who offer you cigarettes. I've never been in a room with a pot smoker who didn't want me to smoke with him. Also heavier more expensive drugs. Nobody is more generous than a user. They want you to do it with them, they want company in badness. Ernie is excited by the idea of making me complicit, as if he were taking my cherry.

Feb. 11, '61

Bought chestnuts, put them in the oven, turned up the heat, and after a while went to see how they were coming along. When I opened the oven door the chestnuts exploded in my face. I forgot to slice them. I looked into the heart of the explosion and saw the lines of force as the chestnuts, suddenly torn apart, sent bits of meat and shell streaking away in all directions. The lines were like spokes radiating from the hub of a wheel, or spears of starlight.

Mar. 1, '62

I arrive at the Port Authority terminal at seven A.M. and get on the number thirty bus to Paterson, New Jersey. The bus goes through the Lincoln Tunnel, then Secaucus and Rutherford, and passes Fairleigh Dickinson University. At 7:25 I'm in Paterson, and walking up a long hill with my fat briefcase bumping the side of my leg. I get to my class at eight A.M. Standing outside the room, smoking a cigarette, I heard a student say, "He's outside, smoking." I put out the cigarette. I was still feeling unsettled, but walked into the room and began the class. I said I will read one of their compositions aloud and stop at the end of every sentence that has a problem, and I will ask them to tell me what is wrong with the sentence and they can't look at it. They had to listen. I told them to hear what is wrong. I told them you must learn to hear. You can't read or write with your eyes. You go to movies with your eyes, and when you come out you are always dumber than when you went in.

Friends and acquaintances teach at Columbia—Allen Bergson, Ross Firestone, Richard Brett, Fred Grab, Edward Said. I'll never have a Ph.D.

My Paterson colleagues complain about the low quality of the students, and talk about the purpose of teaching. Zale said he just failed half of his students. Said he searched his soul for a way not to do that, but there was finally nothing else he could do except fail them, including a student who had received an A last semester. Zale then said he learned that the student got a C in another course, "a very low C," and that relieved him a little of his doubts. It supported his decision to fail the student. Much deliberation is required and much has to be said on the subject of grading these poor little ignorant kids from the sticks. New York is fourteen miles away. From a hilltop on campus you can see the Manhattan skyline. Most of these kids have never been there.

There was something physically intimidating in the way Zale asked for my agreement. He leaned at me and a vein bulged in his neck. His mouth is big, his forehead high and boney, and his wrists are wide. He talked about the importance of grammar as if it were a moral vision. He had taught junior high school for twelve years before he got this job at Paterson, and says that he teaches grammar with pleasure. I never teach grammar. I probably couldn't. English grammar is Latin grammar, imposed by nineteenth-century scholars, neither natural nor appropriate to English. Why teach it to kids who, for the most part, are incapable of learning it? The gorgeous Italian girls who sit in the front row and cross and uncross their legs all during the hour couldn't care less. Maybe I should be like Zale, and teach them grammar.

The way the professors talk. A hundred words where one or two would be enough, and they give odd emphases to words as words, as if words are about words more than anything else. They begin to seem material, like coins or cookies.

The sentences grow heavier, thicker, and much longer than they have to be, as if in the hope that significance, like yeast, will rise from the slow dough of the words. The professors have a few ideas, but no thoughts. The ideas pop up according to the occasion, but they never have thoughts, only small recognitions which lead to ideas. Oh, you mean that idea. I know that idea. Well then, here is this idea: "Yikkipickywickylaslatttummuckyblabobbleclop." If they didn't have ideas, they might say things worth saying. Plato's philosopher kings practice the dialectic. They abide in an infinite flow of thoughts.

Mar. 6, '61
Sylvia said adolescent love is extremely physical because of the social taboos which are taken far more seriously in adolescence than later. Later, when we become indifferent to the taboos, physical passion diminishes. I agreed, but said the taboo was a thing *despite which* kids make love and so gain intensity of feeling (like self-pity?) because they're giving something up for each other. Later, when the taboo is forgotten, there is nothing to give up except the body. Per-

versions are invented to recapture the original heat thrill. I was carried away by the sudden access of total illumination. I was flying. You have to give something up, I said, but after you've done everything sexual you don't have anything to give up. Sylvia's face darkened. She was angry. Conversation wandered off toward literary things. We had different interpretations of *Death in Venice,* but didn't argue about them. She let me know how much it irritates her when I talk down to her. After she said it, I wondered if it were true that I talked down to her. It seemed I talked only the way I used to talk to Allen. Then I supposed it didn't matter how it seemed to me. I asked if she thought I was stupid. She said no. I felt embarrassed. The subject changed to what she intended to buy when she went out—brassieres—and that changed to the great subject of a wedding dress—and now she insisted that I come with her. I wanted to work on the story for which I still felt something, though less than before, but I didn't *not* want to go shopping with her. I said a few half-ass things intended as no, I'm not going, but not final things. I said I needed a shave, was reluctant to walk into a ladies' store looking like a bum. She said it wouldn't matter. I shaved and we went. It was very very windy and cold along MacDougal Street. She said she hadn't realized how cold it was. If she had, she said, she wouldn't have insisted that I come with her.

I remembered a party in a house outside of Ann Arbor. There was a jazz band—piano, bass, drums, and sax—playing in one of the large rooms. A heavy odor of marijuana hung in the air. The host appeared now and then looking pleased, as if he liked seeing strangers in every room, the party out of his control. It wasn't wild, but with a constant flow of people who knows what they're doing. It became late and I was a little drunk, wandering from one part of the house to another. I entered a long hall and was surprised by the silence, as if I had entered another house.

A girl at the other end of the hall was walking toward me. I saw large blue eyes and very black hair. She was about average height, doll-like, features delicate as cut glass, extremely pretty, maybe the prettiest girl I'd ever seen. When she came up to me I took her in my arms and kissed her. She let it happen. We were like creatures in a dream. Holding her hand, I drew her with me and we passed through rooms where people stood about, and then left the house. As we drove away she said her name was Margo. She was a freshman at the university, from a town in northern Michigan. I took her home. It was obvious that she'd never gone home with a man. She didn't seem fearful, only uncertain, the question in her eyes: "What happens next?" What happened next was nothing much. We fell asleep in our clothes. I wasn't the one to make her no different from everyone.

Sylvia hated every dress she tried on. I hated them, too, and she could see it in my expression and took it personally. She was very angry, but said nothing when we left the store, and it was too cold outside for her to make a scene. We walked with our heads down and hands in our pockets, saying nothing. At the 8th Street Bookstore, where we went inside to warm up and browse, I ran into Eddie Epstein. He was interested in chatting. I was, too, but reluctant to say much because I couldn't invite Eddie up to our apartment. He'd see the revolting condition in which I live, maybe mention it to his mother, and there'd be gossip. Sylvia came up to us. I introduced her and she nodded shyly and smiled, then wandered off down an aisle of books, out of sight, hiding as usual. She didn't want to meet anybody. I couldn't even suggest we all go somewhere for coffee. Eddie had read one of my stories in a literary magazine, and referred to the characters as "grotesques." I was surprised. The characters seemed to me like people I know.

Mar. 7, '61

Ernie's stock crashed. He lost everything he'd invested, most of it borrowed money. He is in great debt. I asked why he didn't sell before it crashed. He said he couldn't. "The stock was still going up." I said, "You knew it would crash." He said, "I couldn't sell it." I saw his face in the sound of his voice, the ironical smile in his heavy rosy lips. He's a big soft woman. He'd conned himself, and was no different from investors completely in the dark. He'd become a believer, and had a seizure of masochistic self-annihilation. The stock crashed. He knew it would happen. He let it happen to himself.

Mar. 9, '61

Went to dinner at the bocce restaurant, a family-run place. We feel respectful of traditional Italian life, how they gather to eat and smoke, and how the men play bocce. When Sylvia took off her coat a cockroach jumped out of it and ran up the wall. She was mortified.

The Italian girl has olive skin, light brown hair, and green eyes. She sits in the front row, to my left, a few chairs from the door. It is impossible to see her all at once. I look at her hair and I see it, but then lose it as I look away to her eyes or legs. She's one creature, but her elements forbid dissolution into unity. Like Italy—her elements—eyes, lips, nose, fingers, knees—like towns and cities—while visiting one, you can't think of another.

In my elementary school, P.S. 188, at the corner of Monroe and Market streets, teachers screamed at the kids and sometimes hit them. Elaine talked back to Miss Higgins, a big hitter. We were about ten years old. Elaine's mother came to the classroom. She sided with Miss Higgins, demanding that Elaine apologize for having talked back. She wouldn't. Her mother slapped her face. Elaine remained silent and took the abuse, as if she would sooner be beaten to death than concede to them. I was terrified, and sick with love because Elaine had short black curly hair and pale white skin, and was very pretty and bright. When I came out of school, my mother would be waiting for me at the corner, across Market Street. She'd never have hit me in front of Miss Higgins, not even if she believed I'd been rude. My mother was much better than Elaine's or anyone's.

April 1, '61
Ernie calls, says he is in big trouble. He owes money to "the mob." He was laughing, a sick frightened whiny laugh. He wanted to ask me to lend him money, but the request was made in the strangest halfhearted way, more like a feeble suggestion than a request, as if he realized before he finished asking that it was ridiculous, and then he changed the subject. If he must turn to me for money, he is truly desperate. I wish I could feel deeply concerned or even feel pity—not that it would make any difference. The minute I hang up the phone I forget about him, except for a lingering sense that I owe him something more than conversation, but now I'm not even thinking of him, only this anxiety—owing more than I could give. He once walked into my bedroom without knocking. Roslyn happened to be standing beside the bed half dressed. She put her hands on her hips and turned to look at Ernie. He blushed and made some idiotic remark as he backed out of the room. She didn't seem embarrassed, but coolly indignant. Ernie walked in because, subconsciously, he wanted my girl. With Ernie I have always had the sense that he wants something from me, but not anything I can give him, like beautiful Roslyn, money, or love. Even when he was giving me the tip on the market, I knew he wanted something.

When Ernie cooked a steak, he'd squeeze a tube of anchovy paste onto the steak. When he saw me staring at him he would blush. The big face became pink and florid, and he looked like a hothouse lily, smooth-skinned, meaty, with large juicy brown eyes. He blushed as if ashamed, but he was only mildly embarrassed and tickled by his eccentricity. Couldn't deny himself excess. "Would you like some steak?" he'd ask in a jocular tone. I'd say, "No, thanks." He'd then eat enthusiastically, taking huge mouthfuls, making a show of how he relishes steak smeared with anchovy paste. He knew he was disgusting. He didn't enjoy anything, not even steak. The enjoyment, the satisfaction, the sufficiency Ernie needs isn't in the sensual universe. He couldn't deny himself excess even when he knew the stock would crash.

DRAWING BY
SYLVIA BLOCH.

We moved from MacDougal Street to an apartment on 104th Street, near Columbia University, where Sylvia attended night school. She took a class in German, thinking she might someday do graduate work and would have to pass exams in modern languages, but she had no idea of what subject she would study, and soon gave up German as well as night school.

April 13, '62

Driving back to Manhattan three days a week with William J. Stone, a cop, thirty-eight years old, who has a kind of worldly wisdom, a sense of decorum, and maintains some formal tone in conversation since I'm a "Professor," but says he could tell I'm different, not "really one of our little community." He didn't specify how I am different. He works a full day and goes to school. Hardly sleeps. Has five children. His wife is a teacher. He asserts his presence in class, asking sensible questions, argues with the essays we're reading, puts me on the spot. He is a Catholic but has liberal sentiments, reads the *New York Post* occasionally and likes Murray Kempton's column. Takes calls at the police station and dispatches cars to answer complaints. Says he doesn't like to send cars to marital disputes. Too dangerous. But if a child calls and says the mother and father are fighting, he will send a cop. He can't bear the thought of a child in pain.

I drive to school with Sam, who is completing his Ph.D. at Columbia. He likes to talk about his lovers, and is always high-spirited, personal, and amusing. I'd never talk about a woman the way he talks about men—the intimate physical details. He knows somebody whose lover demanded that he wear braces and rubber bands, and he found a dentist who would do it. The braces were painful and looked hideous, and food got stuck in them. His lover thought they were sexy. I don't know men who talk that way about women, or about what they find sexually exciting. Sam said of a new lover, "I like his cock."

If Sylvia weren't opposed to meeting new people, I'd invite Sam to dinner. He'd have to sit on the couch with us, which is our bed, and eat precooked cheese noodles, which is often our dinner. When my old buddy Mel came to lunch, Syliva cooked sole, even adding grapes as suggested in the cookbook. Maybe because Mel is a psychiatrist, she felt intimidated. She cooked with fury and hatred. She resents and detests cooking, but thinks it's her job. It's O.K. if I shop, clean the house, take out the garbage and laundry, and go to work, but cooking for company is her job and she has done it one time. My mother cooks and cooks. She sends us packages of gefilte fish and mandelbrot and other things Sylvia loves to eat, though not without resentment.

April 23, '62

Came home and found Ellen in the living room, sitting on the floor near Sylvia, who was sprawled on the couch, and both girls spoke in slow, sluggish voices and seemed vaguely bemused, but I made nothing of it until an hour later when I noticed the stub of a cigarette in an ashtray. Both were stoned, pretending to be normal as we talked, since they knew I disapproved. I found myself thinking it was sweet and sensuous and erotic, two stoned slender girls, same height and build, one dark and the other blond, telling each other about their adventures as the light became Manhattan gray. They hadn't turned on any lamps, just smoked their cigarettes and let it happen.

June 9, '62

Ernie killed himself.

May 10, '63

The old major came in to see what grade I'd given him. I said, "I gave you a D." He began to break up, his head turning right and left as if executing formal military postures. His body remained loose, hands flapping, half-waving, as he said, "Aw gee. Jesus. You can't. I can't get a D. My other marks . . ." and his head kept turning right and left. I interrupted him to make his head stop. "You did badly in your other classes?" as if that mattered, and then I thought the grade I gave him doesn't matter either. He said, "Yeah. Aw, Mr. Michaels." I said, "You failed the final." I'd been generous giving him a D. I supposed I could be more generous. He was twitching helplessly. I said, "All right, I'll give you a C," and looked away. He muttered, "Do you know my name?" I said, "Yeah," to the desktop, not him. He whispered, as if scared of breaking a spell, "Joseph Conte."

After Conte, Dora arrives and says in her hushed nervous voice, "I was afraid, ashamed, afraid to talk to you, but I heard from Mr. Fulton you were interested in seeing me, so I came." Later, Fulton lumbers over for the dirt, but I was vague, having not much to say. With Dora I was bored and annoyed. How did Fulton get the idea that I was interested in talking to her? I was going to give her a failing grade in two classes. Seeing her show up for the final exam was irritating because, according to my liberal policy, attendance doesn't matter. If she did well on the final, I'd have to give her a good grade. But attendance does matter in her case because she was never there at all, or hardly ever, and I wanted to give her an F. I showed her the grade sheet for Advanced Composition with her name and the F beside it. Her eyes popped and she gasped, seemed nearly to leer because her grin was so sudden and wild. I asked if she were failing out of school on purpose and she said, "Yes and no," and then said things were impossible at home and she was going to court that night. What for? I don't know, didn't ask. The point—as far as she's concerned—is that she is a small girl, pockmarked, nearsighted, and smart enough to know she's not a good student, so why shouldn't she fail out and go to court? She said she was also screwing up everything else, and she was interested in "broad strokes," great self-destructive actions. I asked what there was for her to screw up now that she had finished with school, and she said, "Someone's life, perhaps." One life, her own, was easy. Two would be an achievement. She said that she'd almost done it with someone, but the person grew frightened and quit at the last minute. Done what?

May 15, '63

Allen is out of town, so Brett phones. The usual conversation, full of my anxious suggestions about what we might do that evening, and Brett's gasps and strained constipated silences. We agree to meet at his apartment. Sylvia has been reading *Wuthering Heights* and nei-

ther needs nor wants me around. The door was double-locked
when I returned, which is a statement. She's in love with Heathcliff.

At Brett's apartment he told me that he'd discovered more homosexual material in Shakespeare's *Lucrece,* and he is contemplating a
book on the subject but isn't yet quite sure. When he is, I think they
will carry him off. While Brett talked he drew his feet up on the
couch, hooking the edge with his heels, and spread his legs so that
I was obliged to look at his crotch. I tried not to think this was a
gross baboonlike sexual overture, and not to think the obvious fact
about Brett. I rattled on about Antonioni and Truffaut movies,
making conversational noises, and eventually he closed his legs and
then we went out for sandwiches. He was for going to The Stage;
I was for The Tip Toe Inn because Sylvia thought she might join
us and, for her convenience, I wanted to be nearby. Tip Toe Inn it
was. Brett said he'd lost much weight and he checked the menu for
things to make him fat. He chose meatballs and potatoes. During
the meal he asked about my homosexual friend at work, what he
told me, and how detailed it was. He wanted to hear it all. I told him
what I remembered. He was titillated. After the meal I called Sylvia
for the second time. She said she didn't want to go out, and then
said I sounded glad. Brett said, "Let's walk down West End so I can
smoke a cigarette," which means marijuana. I said I thought he was
going to cut that out. He said he'd been on cocaine lately. He'd told
me that before and said that it was awful. Now he said it was grand.
"You get further and further out. On other things you just go up.
When coke wears down it takes just another sniff to send you off
again." We went to a movie, *Hud,* and then he made two phone
calls and we separated. Apparently he was going to get more cocaine, and he'd been thinking about it all evening. He said during
dinner that he'd been "thinking about giving money to a girl."
"Keeping her?" I asked. I think he said no, but his response was so

vague I can't be sure. It didn't occur to me that he was talking about a prostitute.

He seems to want to tell me something, but also not to want to tell me, and seems to enjoy the tension between telling and not telling. We didn't talk at all in the taxi to the restaurant. The movie was boring at times. Walking in the street was nearly impossible. We can't walk together. He either leans on me or falls behind in the crowd. We can't manage to cross the street at the same time. Saying goodnight was clumsy, stiff, and dissatisfying. We were standing six feet apart. People actually passed between us. He said he would call and nodded questioningly, as if he weren't sure he would call or that I wanted him to call. I nodded back and waved, desperate to get away. I smoked incessantly during the evening. The turkey sandwich was all right. My dessert, blueberry pie, was gummy and too sweet. The twilight air was balmy and, if not for being in the city, I'd have loved the quality of the evening and the night. Instead I had the anxious sense that somewhere outside the city lies happiness and time is passing. I was standing on the sidewalk trying to say goodnight to the most neurotic man in the United States of America, with people hustling by and time passing and I had the painful sense that this isn't necessary. I could be happy if I were far away from here.

May 26, '63
Possible story: Agatha gave an expensive dress to Pat, a girl she met in the madhouse. Later Agatha decided she wanted the dress back. Pat said it's the nicest dress she ever had, and she could never afford to buy one like it while Agatha could buy one anytime. Agatha said, "All right, keep the dress," but then, weeks later, during an argument she said, "Give me my dress, I'm going." Agatha told Sylvia a similar story about having given a blouse to a woman who then got married, moved to Long Island, and disappeared from Agatha's life.

Agatha decided one day that she wanted the blouse to cut up and use the material for something else. She went to a lot of trouble to run the woman down and spent a day traveling to Long Island and back just to retrieve the blouse. I tried to imagine why she did it, what was her motive. She can afford a thousand blouses. When they put her in the madhouse, it was a classy madhouse in the center of Manhattan. Sylvia was resentful because nothing that luxurious was available to her. The madhouse seemed glamorous, romantic, very desirable. She envied Agatha's lunacy, or at least the idea of it, as well as her money.

June 9, '63

Bernie came by at eleven and sat for two hours in the straight-backed wooden chair. It is an extremely uncomfortable chair. He neither complained nor moved to another chair. The essential city friend who suffers and doesn't complain. I was concerned, but didn't know what to say and wondered if Bernie was sitting there to make me uncomfortable. After Bernie left I remembered to carry out the garbage. The kitchen had begun to stink. The stink stayed. I returned with magazines that I found near the garbage cans. I read the magazines and Sylvia read the magazines, as if we were very interested in them, though neither of us has ever bought a magazine. We listen to the radio talk shows late at night. Once, a man arguing with the host, said very seriously, "You have missed the whole boat." We began giggling and hugging each other. We loved the comment and said it to each other hundreds of times, "You have missed the whole boat," lying on the couch in the darkness, the radio playing long into the night.

I tried to doze. Couldn't. Got up and washed all the dirty dishes. Went into the back room to look at the writing. Became depressed. Sylvia came in to get a blanket. She was in her underpants. I went into the living room after her and lay down with her. She was read-ing *Jane Eyre*. I kissed her. She complained. I got up. She said, "See, you don't want to sleep with me." To sleep with the light on while she's reading isn't sleeping with her. I couldn't possibly explain that without embarrassment.

Tomorrow I go downtown to see my parents and help pack for their move to the new apartment near the barbershop. It's on the fourteenth floor and has a terrace and a view. "It's too high to see anything," says my mother. You could say, "It's high enough to see everything," but she means you have to be near the street. See people. A view is meaningless to her if she can't see people. She takes no pleasure in a view for its own sake. From a mountaintop or the rim of the Grand Canyon or the roof of the Empire State Building—views that would thrill others—would seem to her ab-stract, grandiose, boring. People who like a view, or great vistas empty of people, need it to set off their sense of themselves. The sight of people takes something from the sublimity of isolation and loneliness, the thrill of oneself as the sole sensate object, the view being an abstraction. Abraham travels three days through a landscape without description. He doesn't notice anything. Eleanor Klein said that I could walk into a room where two midgets were fuck-ing on the floor and I'd step over them and walk by. I'm like Abra-ham. I notice nothing.

Josie phoned. She wanted to go to the movies. I said no. I was abrupt and flat because I've known her all my life. With an ac-quaintance, I'd never have spoken like that. This time I hurt her feelings. Then she wouldn't answer my questions about her job. I tried to keep her talking and make up for my rudeness. I couldn't say I'm sorry, or say things are bad here and when the phone rang and I heard her voice I couldn't suppress my frustration and I spoke as if she were responsible. I invited her to come over and said Bernie will be here. She said no. I then felt worse, bad-guilty. She's alone on Saturday night. Cooks dinner for herself. Her job ends in three months, and she doesn't want to start looking for another job. She wanted this job very much, they gave it to her, but there was no job. She had to pester them, but why did they give it to her? To see if there was a job? They gave it to her because they liked her, but there wasn't any job. That's how life is for Josie. Looks, brains, and talent, but there is nothing for her to do. She's nice but nobody has anything for her to do. I want to tell her to change. I want to make her understand. She musn't go about with ideals that have no relation to anything. They gave her the job because she already had so much, as if they said, "All right, here is nothing." Now she really has nothing and phones to ask if I want to see a movie. I said no. I feel horrible.

June 10, '63
Agatha came by, apparently upset. She had to talk to Sylvia privately. Later Sylvia told me that Agatha's father seduced her girlfriend. Agatha must have known that Sylvia would tell me. She tells Sylvia stories that are luridly sensational, painful, humiliating, etc., all the while knowing Sylvia will tell me. Maybe it adds to the frisson of telling if she knows that I'll hear it, too. No. While telling she must imagine it's just between herself and Sylvia. Neither of us would tell anyone the stuff she tells Sylvia. I feel guilty even writing about it.

Bernie came by and talked about a fight he saw on TV, the number of beers he drank, and movies he's seen lately, telling me all the plots, and then talked about someone at work who reads slowly and doesn't finish the book. He talked about beautiful actresses, his idea for a children's book, and made wisecracks. His teasing feels more hostile than funny. I say something in one spirit, he takes it in another and giggles. Ernie used to ask me, since Bernie is brilliant, how we could use him to get rich.

Brett and Allen came by very late and sat in the living room and smoked. There was enormous tension for no reason except that Brett, with his rigid posture and half-smile, exuded weird ambiguities and tension. He is pale and skinny, and he wears a jacket, white shirt, and tie, his classroom outfit. All of us were affected by his tension. We talked until after three A.M., mainly about Shakespeare's sonnets, which Brett thinks are full of images of sexual perversions. He quotes a line and then waits for one of us to say what he thinks is in the line. While he waits, his eyes dart from Sylvia to me to Allen, and he smiles and is barely able to repress his laughter. I never know what Brett thinks is funny, but then none of us imagines the things he imagines. Long tense minutes pass before Brett says the line is about masturbation or some sort of anal eroticism. I expect his interpretation to take that direction, but I'm never able to anticipate it, and I don't see it in the line even after he points it out.

June 11, '63
Every day brings information: Brett's drug habit and dangerous strolls along Riverside Drive late at night; Josie's job; Bernie's movies and job applications and letters of rejection; Sylvia's ideas about me and the novels she's reading. Yesterday I said it was great to receive so much information, so much of it personal. I felt like a psychiatrist, deeply privileged. Bernie said, "But knowing so much leads to hopelessness, a conviction of the impossibility of change." He wasn't joking for once.

Seymour told me that he saw a psychiatrist for three years. During their last session he told the psychiatrist about a dream in which Seymour had dealings with a small man. The psychiatrist asked who the man might be, and Seymour then realized the man in the dream was the psychiatrist. The psychiatrist stood up. He was well over six feet tall. For three years—an hour-long session two times a week—Seymour assumed that his psychiatrist was a small man, about five feet four, shorter than Seymour. In fact he was almost a foot taller. I thought it was a hilarious story. How people see you— commonly, ordinarily—is distorted by needs and fears. They see you as tall when you're short, mean when you're kind, contemptuous when you're admiring, sexually aggressive when you're indifferent. The aggressive woman who came on to me said I'd been flirting with her. I asked, "How had I been flirting?" She said, "With your eyes, your voice, your movements." I didn't even like her, but maybe her impression was healthy; she found herself desirable.

June 12, '63

Went to a class in American lit. at Columbia. The professor had a British accent. He was scattered and casual, and apologized for the literature, then for his opinions of the literature, and then he apologized for the shortness of the summer term. If he doesn't like the literature, why is he teaching it, let alone worried about how little time he has to teach it? I live that way, too, doing what I don't want to do. I should be sympathetic. Hypocrisy is a deep condition, and you can't see through yourself. You're helpless to be better than you are.

Can't write. Everything seems thin and unhappy and cold. Not cold passion, just cold and dry as if I'm afraid to let go. It's mid afternoon. The street is quiet, and I'm quiet in this room. The pen slips from my hand and drops onto the table, and I jump.

I should leave town. At least there will be possibilities. Have accomplished nothing. I have no work, no marriage, no friends, no life. A miserable past, an unbearable present, and a grim future unless I go away.

June 14, '63
Phone calls from Donna, Steve, Ross, and Baiba. My parents never call anymore. Oswald called to say he intends to acknowledge me in a book he is writing, or editing—I'm not sure—on Shakespeare. Did I ever say anything to Oswald about Shakespeare? I nearly pleaded with him not to mention my name, but that seemed preciously self-involved, worse than saying nothing. Besides, he'd want to discuss it, and I don't really know why I should care one way or the other. He was being generous, making me feel I'm something I'm not. He thought he was being generous, anyway. No, he thought I would think he was being generous. He thought I would think he was being generous while he actually benefited from the use of my name, though it is of no use to anyone, not even to me.

Saw a movie in which a priest who is a hateful, hating person is loved in a slavish way by a woman who is drab, exceedingly tense, ironic, bitter, self-humiliating, and yet—strangely enough—quite strong. (What is it about this combination that holds my interest? Is this man and woman combination the expressive "thing"? The "thing," in the Henry James sense, the thing most representative of us, or of our time. It matters not one damn what I think, or seem to think, but I go on as if I know otherwise, as if it matters what I think, and as if I have always known that, but it isn't as if it were me that I am talking about.) The woman and the priest have a long curious talk. In a burst of exasperation the priest tells her that he finds her impossible because of her complaints, her period, chilblains, shyness, and timidity. He says that in her effort to be a good woman she is a merely ridiculous parody of his dead wife. She tells him he will die hating. He gets up and starts to leave, then stops, returns, and asks her if she is coming. She says yes. So that's life in Sweden. They say so little that the little they say matters immensely. But why do they say so little? There was no plot. There was one short sequence that ends in suicide. A man kills himself and his wife says, "Then I am alone?"

After the movie we walked up Third Avenue to a flashy hamburger place full of kids. We had hamburgers, onion rings, and coffee. I wanted to talk about the movie, but Sylvia wouldn't. So we talked about where we will sit, counter or booth? and then we talked about who in the room is gay, which was ridiculous. Almost everyone was gay. Then Sylvia said, "Doesn't this hamburger taste good?" She refused to talk about the movie, though we talk constantly about movies or books when people visit and sit in our living room all night. With me alone she decides to talk like an idiot.

I woke with the sun in my eyes, still dressed except for my shoes. Sylvia said, "The sun is out," then complained about how we don't go out to sit in the sun. We slept some more, then woke about nine thirty. I'm writing a story which includes autobiographical facts. Some of it is imagined, but not enough, so it's not real writing. I worked hard, but I'll throw it away eventually.

Sylvia asked if I get headaches in the back of my head, and seemed to want me to say yes so I did. She then told me about an article she'd read about teenagers and their back-of-the-head headaches which are caused by a slipped disk near the top of the neck, and can be cured by exercise or surgery. I ought to see a doctor, she said. I wasn't willing to see a doctor. She railed about my willingness to suffer, not even to do simple exercises. For an instant I thought she wanted me to have headaches and then remembered I had said that I had them. Bernie called, thank God, before she lost control and spiraled into violence. She went out to play Ping-Pong with Bernie.

Then Seymour Kleinberg called. I was in the bathroom. I hurried to the phone before it stopped ringing, but was hardly able to talk. Seymour could tell I was low, though I tried to disguise it. He said he'd call back. I wanted to talk to him, but I couldn't think. Depression stupefies.

Something inside my shoe was sticking my foot. I had to sit down and take off my shoe. I sat on a bench at the 103rd Street subway station, next to a Negro lady. The thing in my shoe was a pebble. It took minutes to slide it up and out of my sock by pinching it and shoving it gradually along the top of my foot, then ankle, and then lowering the sock—the suspense was terrific—and plucking it out just before the train arrived. I was concerned about the lady's feelings every minute, which I wouldn't have been if she were white. I had a pebble in my sock. It had nothing to do with race relations, but these days you have to think, which already feels wrong, or racist, no matter how pure you are in heart.

I walked east along 58th Street to the Plaza. Sylvia told me on the phone that she had bought a mahogany salad bowl for seventeen dollars, and a new hat. Also a new can opener, guaranteed forever. It cost two dollars, the hat cost three. She looked beautiful in the hat. Altogether, in her black dress and black hat, she looked glamorous and idiosyncratic. She was self-conscious and happy. I saw her sitting on a bench beside an old couple. She was wearing the hat, and had the large paper-wrapped package containing the bowl on her lap, and she was trying to light a cigarette but the wind was too strong. I sat about fifty feet away on the rim of the fountain until she noticed me, and then I waved and she smiled. I walked over to her and lighted her cigarette. "You look beautiful," I said. She said that a man pointed to her in the street and said, "You—you—you in some play."

June 15, '63

Spent much of the day with Seymour and talked to him about friends, and my hurt feelings. He said we were passive types, he and I, and that we got exactly what we allowed our friends to give us. If you allow it, they will take extreme liberties, and they will even be cruel as if it were natural and expected of them. He then said he would tolerate nothing of the kind again, and that he would speak up immediately if there were any sign of hostility from a friend. He spoke quickly and sounded passionate on the subject, and then said he was miserable and he joked about looking forward to old age and death. He talked about his mother—her inability to show love, and her not making him welcome when he visited, but, instead, expressing accumulated resentment for his not having visited sooner. He said he has adopted a realistic method of handling her whining accusations. He tells her the truth bluntly. When she goes into an act of indifference to his visit, he responds with indifference, thus expressing his real feelings, the feelings she deserves from him, and said he gets satisfaction by surprising her this way and frustrating her effort to produce guilt in him. He laughed saying all this and glanced at me as if to see whether I approved or maybe just agreed. Later he talked about a child whose parents hadn't wanted him, and the child was going to grow up and be unlovable, and that it wasn't fair because a child is defenseless against adults, and they had no right to treat him that way. When I talked to Sylvia about Seymour, she said that I aggrandize my friends, and in general I always make things more exciting and valuable than they are. She said this because she suspected that I am fond of Seymour. Lou Walls said something like that about me, too. "You are the harbinger of all our virtues." Sylvia said that my description of Alex Bespaloff as a wine and food expert was a lie, though he is both. She can't bear the idea that Alex is just what I said. I didn't see any point in arguing with her. We walked alongside the river, and I walked along the edge, outside the fence. She said I was being a showoff and a sadist, willfully frightening her. I kept on doing it and didn't enjoy it at all.

June 16, '63

Went to the bar mitzvah of Sylvia's relative. Organ music, hidden choir, two rabbis. The rabbis used a pulpit, facing the congregation except when the Torah was displayed. The congregation was an audience, the rabbis entertainers. One sat through most of the ceremony. The other stood at the pulpit reading and singing. Both wore thick glasses with shining silvery frames. Neither had a beard or long sideburns; they were dressed like bishops with pointed hats and long priestly robes. Occasionally the rabbi sang with great feeling, as if parts of the service meant more to him than others. The Torah was sheathed in red velvet. On the velvet, in gold letters, it said "In memory of . . ." and looked like an advertisement. The pointer was highly polished, elaborately wrought silver over a foot long. The rabbi who sang had a good voice. He frowned while singing and moved his lips into carefully shaped circles, triangles, and squares appropriate to particular notes. He fondled the notes with his mouth, savored them. Eyes, large and black, remained unblinkingly on the congregation. The rabbi's white shirt collar and large V-knotted tie showed above his black robe. Black well-groomed hair streaked with gray. The other rabbi had gray, almost white, hair, crew-cut, vigorously thick-bristled. Both were youthfully energetic, well fed, sensuous. Their hand movements were highly controlled, perfectly modulated and timed. The performance was professional, sharp, without religious feeling—just feeling, like a Broadway show, neither unserious nor deep. I preferred my father's shul on the Lower East Side, old rabbis davening, women gathered in the balcony, creaking floors, odors of ancient plumbing. More real.

June 17, '63

Went downtown to my parents' with Sylvia and packed another box of books, and seemed to eat for hours, and then watched television until one in the morning. Sylvia went to sleep. I thought it wouldn't be bad to own a television set. I'd watch it until I was very old and died in the middle of some show, painlessly, eyes still open, appearing no different to anyone, not even myself. Television makes brain death all right. I feel good in my parents' apartment. Sylvia didn't complain about anything, and didn't accuse them or me of anything.

I painted some pictures. They stink, but, while painting, I take them seriously. I paint while company is here. I don't enjoy company anymore. Nothing feels natural or good except visiting my parents downtown and sitting like a dolt in their living room, watching some degrading television program while my mother, flushed with menopause, ministers to my needs with coffee, fruit, and cake. My father snoozes in his chair. I look up now and then, fearfully, to see if his shirtfront pulses so that I can be sure he is alive.

Possible story: A gourmet type on an eating trip in an exotic environment, alone, dedicated to self-indulgence, a life of continuous and unqualified pleasure. He overeats, gets sick, and starts thinking he might die in his hotel room—the pains, the vomiting, the diarrhea—the drama becomes another pleasure. Actually, I'm thinking about Ernie, his peculiar nature. I see him as if he were still alive and in this room. If someone is wearing a beautiful tie, Ernie thinks his own tie is ugly. A friend shows up at a party with a pretty girl, Ernie feels ashamed of his girl. Ernie orders a meal in a restaurant, and when the waiter carries a different order to the neighboring table Ernie loses his appetite. It doesn't matter what the different order might be. It's different, and that's enough to make him feel he ordered the wrong dish. His own possessions, like his clothes from the best stores in Chicago, made Ernie envious. Handmade British shoes, classy luggage—his finest things suggested to him that others have finer, more expensive things. Regardless of what he owned, he never had anything worth a damn. Ernie could never simply be, and now he isn't.

Wanting things makes you crude and unhappy. The compulsive fucker, my old communist buddy Horton, card-carrying member of the "Big C." A scholar, he read voraciously. With books as with girls, insatiable devourer. I was horrified by the girls. Could they be like Horton, shamelessly bestial? Horton said he "serviced" them. Two a day sometimes, and never showered in between. I was horrified, angry, envious. He referred to girls as "dickless wonders." He was elaborately courteous in courtship, a sign of contempt. He read poems to the dickless wonders, and described their ecstasies to me. Men don't talk, except for him. Food, movies, books, sports—all right. Ten thousand women didn't make him a man.

June 18, '63
Rosenthals visited. They brought ice cream. Phyllis was dressed nicely, as if for a date. Bob was winded and sweating, bearded, and looked thinner than the last time I'd seen him. He was funny and brilliant, and did most of the talking. He held forth on "Brettstein" for about twenty minutes, never calling him Brett. He said, "Imagine a Proust who can't write, but he carries his bed with him." He said, "Brettstein had a kind of nobility, and used to write intelligent complicated critical essays. I never could understand them. He chased remarkable girls, and became their mascot. He went out with a girl named Gina who, at the time, was ordinary. He felt nobody liked him for that reason, or liked her. He dropped her. She went to Europe that summer and by the time she returned she had

blossomed. Everyone wanted her. Brettstein was at her wedding with a host of other admirers. She told them one at a time that she might have married them. She told this to Brettstein. It was the big moment of his life."

Rosenthal said he played tricks on Brettstein. Once, while visiting Rosenthal's dormitory room, Brettstein went to the john, and before he returned Rosenthal changed the position of all the furniture in the room and changed his clothes. Brettstein looked worried, but made no comment about how things had changed. He couldn't be sure. Rosenthal said Brettstein couldn't tell which was real, the first or the second room, because he lives in fantasy worlds. The name Brett is one of them. It was gratifying to hear Rosenthal speak of Brett this way, since he'd been so intimidating so often. Rosenthal described him as "small, contracted, and defective," and said, "he chased remarkable women in the hope one day one of them would whip aside the cover and say, 'All right, you've earned it.' "

He talked about Brett's mother, saying she was small, birdlike, not Jewish but indulgent. The brother was healthy. "In that family," he said, "things were portioned out. You get the health. You get the brains." He told a story about spending an evening smoking marijuana with several people. One of them became suspicious and very paranoiac. Rosenthal teased him and he got angry. Rosenthal said, "I'm sorry. I didn't realize you weren't fooling when you were so paranoid." The guy answered, "You're not sincere and I wasn't fooling and I'm not under the influence of marijuana."

Before the Rosenthals arrived, we had a fight and Sylvia took her toothbrush and rushed out as if forever. I went after her a few minutes later and found her on 104th Street and Broadway, stranded. She came back with me, went to sleep, and then woke up in good spirits, affectionate and ready for company. She had rushed out despising me, saying the house was too filthy to be cleaned up for company. This was after she had broken a few things in the bathroom. She said that I just sat there while she had to do everything, though it was still two hours before they arrived. She had to sew her dress, clean, cook. I'd have cleaned and cooked if she wanted me to, and would probably have cleaned anyway whether or not she wanted me to. I'd have been happy to go out for dinner. It's true that I was sitting there reading the newspaper, and that she was sewing hurriedly, unnecessarily feeling great anxiety and pressure. None of the drama was necessary, and none of it was anticipated by me. As always, I was surprised—first by the angry scene and her flight, then by her collapse and then by her awakening full of affection as if nothing had happened earlier, and her good spirits, looking forward to the company as if she'd had no worries about the unclean apartment or dinner.

June 20, '63

Agatha has a boyfriend who works as a dog-walker. He is cruel to the dogs, locks them in a closet—two German shepherds and a poodle—and leaves them there for hours. Agatha describes his cruelty with awe. He is also physically cruel to Agatha, treats her like another dog or worse. She objects to being hit and constantly humiliated. She objects, but I think it's mainly when she tells Sylvia what's going on. She doesn't leave the boyfriend. Every story is the same, though the boys and the humiliations are a little different each time. Masochists always get what they want. Properly understood, it's an expression of power.

July 12, '63

Donna came to visit and brought wine, apparently expecting dinner, but, after drinking some wine, Sylvia fell asleep. Donna and I went out for a walk along Broadway. It was early evening, the air was pleasantly warm and the light was nice. Broadway was crowded with end-of-the-day shoppers and people going to dinner, and I didn't see Craig coming toward me. He tapped me lightly in the stomach as we passed. I doubled over, shocked and frightened, not the least aware of what had happened. Craig said I was walking in a daze. He was my best friend at the High School of Music and Art. I used to see him every schoolday, and frequently at NYU, and I was happy to see him today, though somewhat shaken and it took a moment to recover. He wanted to join us, but had to buy pipe tobacco. I said we'd wait while he bought pipe tobacco. Then we had coffee with him.

While having coffee he started talking about his latest invention, a plot machine that would write stories for him. He sometimes built ingenious machines in high school, tiny cameras, tiny radios, etc. He'd gone to Hunter, the school for gifted kids, as had Sylvia. He was musically talented and could also paint and draw. He could do anything. Nice-looking, fine features, brown skin, a slender build. Coiled spring tension in his posture. His glasses had plain plastic frames. He said the plot machine will write stories, and he will sell them. Donna was appalled. Said people write stories to create art. Craig became angry. He disguised the feeling with a half-smile and chuckle. Said he didn't have the money or the time to create art. Then continued talking about his plan to feed into his machine all the criticism he has ever received in rejection slips, and the machine will avoid errors that he has made in the past, and it will provide (1) interest, (2) suspense, (3) resolution—happy or sad. It can be either he said. I suppose the machine is metaphorical, but it actually exists. It's how he feels about himself. He then talked about a ticket he got for smoking in the subway. Said his pipe was in his jacket pocket and had a lid on it. The lid is used to put out the pipe. "Where were you," he asked the subway cop, "when they beat me up in the alley?" The cop said, "I walk my beat in a military manner." Craig paid a five-dollar fine. As we left the coffee shop he said a man is free if he has money. Where are my paintings? he asked. They are in storage, he answered, because he had to move after paying a raise on the illegal rent charged by his landlord. Growing agitated, he said he'd seen Al, who has the "thing on his face," meaning his beard. Said Al doesn't even have his thesis finished but he has a teaching job. If he, Craig, wanted the job he'd have had to finish two theses and receive two degrees. Said if Al turned brown tomorrow they would throw him out. He was biting on his pipe to keep from screaming. I said, "You're right, Craig." I began walking quickly. Donna said she had to get back to the apartment to receive a telephone call. He shouted after me, asking when I would be leaving for Michigan, and I shouted back, "In a month."

Sylvia is asleep on the couch. Fell asleep after Donna arrived, and has been sleeping and sleeping. Goes no place and hates to answer the phone. Difficult to have people over. She resents my lunches with friends, and listens coldly to my stories about other people or about myself. She sees something negative in the stories, even if it's only my enthusiasm while telling. If I had a little fun or if I enjoy talking about something, it's like a blow against her. I find it embarrassing and very discouraging when I begin to suspect—in the midst of telling her about a funny event—that she thinks I'm telling it to seize center stage, and to deny her the chance to shine. She feels this way even when she and I are the only people in the room, though I've listened to her a million times with interest and pleasure in her wit, her brains, her voice. As far as I know, I'm not doing what she thinks, and just happily babbling. I always assume she's amused, and then realize she isn't amused, only getting more and more bitter and angry, waiting for a chance to say something to bring me down.

Craig reminded Donna of her former lover, also black, also a genius, but he was always noticing undercurrents of hostility in everyone's voice, and was concerned about Donna leaving the apartment, even just to go to school. She would get hit by a car, he thought, or worse, she'd meet old friends. When Donna left him it was in her pajamas in the middle of the night while one of their friends held him down and a taxi waited for her outside.

July 31, '63
The day I left the apartment to go to Grand Central Station, Sylvia prepared sandwiches and a thermos of coffee for me since the train ride was overnight and there might be nothing to eat.

The marriage was never happy but neither of us said a word about divorce and I never mentioned it to my journal, and neither of us even said the word "separation" when I left New York to go to graduate school in Michigan, where I'd studied from 1953 to 1956. Then, hundreds of miles apart, we began to write affectionate letters and to speak frequently on the telephone. I think we were so happy being free of each other that it felt like love. Sylvia had no job and wasn't going to school. In not very long she was inspired to join me in Michigan, where things became as bad as ever, and she returned to New York. Both of us began seeing other people. The marriage was essentially over.

Nov. 22, '63
I was in the Student Union with Burt Welcher when we heard that Kennedy had been shot and killed. We went out and walked alongside campus toward the law school, neither of us saying much. We were about to cross the street when a car turned the corner and cut

in front of us. Burt screamed at the driver, "Must you kill more?" then laughed crazily.

Burt is teaching at a community college in Ypsilanti. In class one evening, a student used the word "function." Burt stopped the class and said, "Sir. Function is pronounced *funk-tee-yon,* with a hard K. Repeat after me, *funk-tee-yon.*" He made the student repeat it several times, then made the class repeat it, chanting together in a strong voice, *"Funk-tee-yon, funk-tee-yon, funk-tee-yon . . ."*

Dec. 15, '63

Burt finds ways to punish people who disturb him. They usually have no idea of Burt's ill will because there is nothing between them aside from Burt's impressions. Somebody might represent something noxious to Burt in how he looks, dresses, talks, etc. Most offensive is what he imagines a person thinks about himself. People sense the strangeness in Burt, though he's funny and charming. He doesn't get invited to parties. I'm his only friend, except for his girlfriend and Bob Stern, a former rabbinical scholar now a graduate student in English. Burt spends a great deal of time alone. He told me that his landlady is a young self-absorbed woman who doesn't say hello and has rigid routines. He was trying to convince me of her bad character. I knew he was about to tell me a story. He said his landlady stepped out of the house every morning to collect the mail from the box just outside the front door. She would be in her nightgown, regardless of how cold it was, and would leave the front door open so that she could dash straight back into the house with the mail. On a murderously cold windy morning when she stepped outside, Burt slipped downstairs and slammed the door shut. He heard her pounding on the door and screaming. The pounding grew weaker and the screaming stopped. Burt watched from behind a curtain as she ran across the street barefoot in her nightgown in the terrible cold, and saw her pounding on the door of another house, where nobody answered, and then run to another house and another door. Burt then snuck out of the house. Nobody would imagine that he'd even been in the house when the door slammed shut and his landlady pounded at the door and screamed. As he told the story Burt seemed to identify with the landlady. His voice became loving as he talked of her shock and suffering, a moment of devastation in an ordinary day. She had no idea why the front door slammed shut. Such a loud boom, as if the door had tried to kill her. Burt's expression was earnest, sincere, full of pity. There was a little tear in his eye. He'd done a mean thing, but truly felt for the landlady.

Dec. 19, '63

I took a walk with Burt along State Street in the late afternoon. When we came to Van Boven's men's store, Burt said, "I need a sweater." The store is one long and fairly narrow aisle. A few yards from the front door in the middle of the aisle, a table was stacked with sweaters. Three salesmen were at the end of the aisle, about twenty feet away, talking and laughing. Burt took off his jacket, picked up a sweater, put it on, then put his jacket back on. We turned and walked out of the store. He'd put on the sweater in clear view of the salesmen, such blatant theft that they didn't see it. Burt thinks few people are interested in anything real. Most require a brutal shock. I believe the same, but I accommodate to the common need for irreality which is basic to social life.

Burt is much more sensitive to irrealities than I am, and could have a career in politics or religion or Hollywood or advertising, if he could keep himself from laughing at people and punishing them. Even if you didn't think much of Kennedy, the assassination is serious for the reason that an enormous number of people think it is.

A few nights later, at a pre-Christmas party, a woman said to Burt, "That's a nice tie." He said, in a shy and modest voice, "Actually this is the lining of another tie." Then he talked about his tweed jacket. He said it comes from Scotland, the city of Tweed, on the river Tweed, where men fish for the tweed they use to make jackets. She let him go on, her face blank and still. She wasn't the least amused, only curious and unable to know what to make of Burt. Her expression was so utterly blank that it seemed she didn't believe he was speaking to her in English, or in any language that she understood. I knew her fairly well, since we'd occasionally meet in the Student Union cafeteria and sit together over coffee. Seeing her reaction to Burt made me feel his strangeness to others, but for some reason I find him simpatico, and he is the only one I know in Ann Arbor with whom I can take long walks and talk and not have to do anything else to keep from becoming bored.

During Christmas in New York, as on every school vacation, I went to see Sylvia. I planned to talk to her about a divorce, but she got drunk, and did all the talking, then left the room and swallowed forty-eight Seconals. I heard her fall in the bathroom. I telephoned the police. They arrived with an ambulance. I rode in it to Knickerbocker hospital and stayed with Sylvia, sleeping in a hallway for several days until I was told she would make it. I went home to take a shower. A few hours later I was called back to the hospital. When I got there my brother told me she'd died. I went to her room as if to see if it were true. Her bed was empty. Things I'd brought her in anticipation of going home had been stolen. I'd never seen such emptiness. Soon afterward I was required to go to the morgue. I asked the coroner why Sylvia had died. He looked startled. "Barbiturates," he said. I remember the funeral service, the rabbi saying Sylvia was twenty-four years old, and then the drive to the cemetery, then standing beside the grave and hearing my father begin to cry, which sounded as if, suddenly, the hard cold silent air had whimpered and leaked.

Feb. 1, '65

Ann Arbor. Reading all night at the kitchen table. High on fatigue, I begin thinking there is a presence in the room, standing behind me in the shadows, looking over my shoulder, reading my book, but I'm reluctant to turn. Too frightening. I'm sure I'll see a bearded man seven feet tall, with an iron helmet and icy green eyes. He is holding a spear. Unable to resist, I turn. I'm right.

Conversation with Bernie comes to mind. I said I'd hate to lose my sight more than any other sense because I'd be unable to read. Hearing, he said, is more important to him. Life would be poor if he couldn't listen to music. I was surprised that he chose hearing. It would be hard to take care of yourself and get around if you can't see—and then I thought I could learn to read braille, and I realized there is no substitute for sound.

I tell a story and friends laugh. "You should write that," they say. But anyone can tell a story. When you write it, even the best story dies a little, and usually more than a little, because writing is obliged to respect logic and grammar, and is nothing like experience. So poets sing.

Storm late at night, heavy rain, a thunderous racket, the windows shaking. I heard my name called. A woman's voice in hell pleading with me to join her. I sat up in bed and listened, and was then too frightened to go back to sleep.

I told Willie Smith that I'd heard a voice. I was laughing at myself. He didn't laugh. He said he'd made an appointment for me with a psychiatrist. I was shocked. He hadn't even asked for my permission. Then I felt ashamed. Willie thinks there is something wrong with me. So do others. I can tell that's what they think, though I can't tell why. I talk, laugh, make jokes, seem normal to myself, and I haven't asked anyone for any kind of help. Willie weighs about two hundred and thirty pounds. He's handsome, very strong, cat-quick, and a football hero. In his eyes, I'm a mental case. He is solid. I'm a mess. I'll go to the appointment with the psychiatrist, though I already feel cured by embarrassment.

Incredible, in these circumstances, that I should want sex. My body is a pig.

"The force that through the green fuse drives . . ." is evil.

Michael and I were walking. He stepped into a stationery store, came right out, and handed me a Mont Blanc fountain pen. He too thinks I'm in a bad way.

Possible story: I'd be on a street corner in Manhattan, or hanging around in a bar, waiting for Delight. She was always late. It was humiliating. I couldn't leave. She might arrive in another minute, another minute, another . . . No walls, no locked doors, nothing to stop me from walking away, but I couldn't. I always waited. It was no pleasure. How does a person know you'll wait? Malcolm made me wait. So did Allen. They were neurotically late. I was neurotically punctual. My punctual nature was a challenge. They had to be late.

When Delight finally arrived I was seething. I decided to teach her a lesson. I made an appointment to meet her at the San Remo and I looked forward to being late, but I had to be certain that she arrived on time. I phoned her repeatedly to remind her of our appointment. It seemed like a joke to her. She had a wild, brilliant laugh. It made me laugh. We laughed together. She said that she was leaving as soon as she hung up the phone. I was in midtown, halfway to the bar. I stopped and phoned again from a drugstore. She hadn't left. We laughed. A bit later I phoned her again from the street to make sure that she had left, but she hadn't. We laughed again. I told her to get going immediately. I was more than halfway to the bar. I phoned her again. No answer. She'd left her apartment. She would walk into the bar any moment. Maybe she was already there. At the idea of her waiting for me, I started giggling and running. I tripped on a crack in the sidewalk. It wasn't a bad fall, but I tore my pants at the knee.

Minutes later I arrived at the bar. She wasn't there. I looked at the clock on the wall. I was twenty minutes early. Impossible. Beyond any rational explanation. I was furious at myself. Torn trousers and bloodied palms. No matter. I ordered a bourbon straight and waited until I stopped shaking, then started to walk out so that I could go away and come back later. It would be embarrassing if she found me in the bar, on time, a humble fool. But if she'd actually left her apartment and gone to the bar, she might have arrived before me and realized her mistake. She might then have been there already and gone away. It would have been my fault, telephoning repeatedly, driving her nuts. I couldn't leave the bar. She'd walk in at any moment, laughing, proud of herself. We'd have a drink, then go to dinner. I couldn't hide the torn pants. I'd make a joke about it. She needn't see my palms, and maybe not notice I was limping.

Feb. 2, '65

Willie's psychiatrist is short and square-shaped, middle-aged, and wears a dark double-breasted suit, white shirt, and tie. He looks like a bureaucrat in a city job, maybe a health inspector. Framed diplomas hang on the wall of his drab gray office, and no other decorations. He used to be an army doctor. I told him I'd heard voices.

Actually only one voice. I said it was my former wife's voice. He asked if I was a homosexual. I wanted to ask if he was brain damaged. Has anyone ever asked a homosexual if he's straight? I told him I like girls and made the point so strongly that I felt homosexual. If you like girls, there is no reason to say it. He was utterly square; it was like talking to a cop. I did nothing wrong, but felt guilty. If a man like this can help me, I'm beyond help and I want no part of it. The cold weather in Michigan is unbearable, as bad as New Jersey. Literally unbearable.

How sensitive to cold I've become.

I have bad dreams. I am afraid to go to sleep.

Friends think there is something wrong with me.

I am taking classes in Old English and Middle English and writing a paper on *Beowulf.*

I went to a party. Everyone was an undergraduate except me. The music was mainly songs by the Beach Boys. I was the oldest one there. Me, dancing to the Beach Boys.
　　I've lost a lot of weight.

Feb. 3, '65
I went out with Clancy, who has a Pre-Raphaelite figure and neck. She plays the French horn and has two little kids who are sublimely beautiful. She says they are the product of two rapes. The first was shortly after her marriage. She was awakened in the middle of the night on a train someplace in Canada and raped by her husband. He also raped her the second time. She says she's been told by a certain man here in Ann Arbor never to have sex if she didn't want to. He

told her this angrily—I could hear him in her voice—after they had had sex and she hadn't liked it and was miserable. She's exceedingly nervous, as if she were being tested every minute when she talks. She says, "You don't need a map of the brain to see that sex is close to violence." It made me think of Weathers. He showed me a whip, a cat-o'-nine-tails, that he himself had made. He said that he brings his whip when he goes to parties. In Ann Arbor, in the Eisenhower era, before the sexual devolution, there was nothing as weird as Weathers. There has been a great change of some kind. I don't much like it, but I can hardly say what it is.

I still have to read twenty novels for my qualifying exam. It's maddening to read not for pleasure but only to finish, expecially Hardy's novels. They refuse simply to go where you know they are going. In James's *The Ambassadors* I counted sixteen uses of the phrase "hung fire" before I stopped reading. I'm a slow reader and there is too much to read, especially this way, without pleasure or interest. The night before he took his law exams, Malcolm read *The Brothers Karamazov*. He failed his exams, but that's the proper spirit in which to read novels.

Feb. 9, '65
Harvey bought a blood-red, almost new Mercedes sports car, and parked it in front of the girls' dorm. He then went into the lounge and played the piano. He intended to ask any girl who stopped to listen if she'd like a ride in his Mercedes. He'd planned this for a long time. While he was playing the piano, a girl stopped to listen. She came right up to the piano and stood there, entranced. Harvey quit playing and snarled, "Would you mind not staring at me?"

Harvey said he met a girl. She was from Ohio. He said she was tall and had long brown hair. He raved about her. I told him I'd met a girl at a party last night. I didn't say that she came home with me, but he wasn't at all interested in hearing about the girl I met, and kept on talking about the girl from Ohio. When Ruth walked in, Harvey looked at her with a weird expression, then left abruptly, before I could introduce him to her. I asked Ruth if she was from Ohio. She said, "How did you know?" She had no recollection of ever having met Harvey.

Feb. 10, '65
Ruth was crying: "I hate my body."

"Why?"

"Because it's alive."

"What do you mean?"

"I'm pregnant."

I asked if she'd tried to get help. She said there was nobody to help her. I asked if she'd told her parents. She said she couldn't do that. I said there must be people who can help her. She had a sister at the university, but her sister couldn't or wouldn't help. I told Ruth to get dressed, as if I'd heard enough and was taking over. "As if," for me, is so close to the real thing it might as well be. She got dressed. I said, "Let's go for a walk." She walked beside me like a robot, saying nothing. We must have looked grim, not touching, not talking. She is willing to do anything I tell her to do, which makes me responsible for her. I think she makes me responsible for her. But it's only by chance that we're together. She might have gone home from the party with some other guy. True, but the fact is I woke up beside her.

I say, "Eat something." She picks up a slice of bread and nibbles listlessly. I say, "Let's go." She stands up to go.

I say, "Do you want to see a movie?" She shrugs, waiting to know if I want to see a movie.

Ruth is now less worried. As if the problem were mine, I'm worried.

I tell myself that maybe Ruth went home with other guys for months before she met me. The fact remains.

Feb. 11, '65

She is tall and broad-shouldered, and has narrow hips, long arms and legs. From the back, she looks boyish and athletic, except for her long wavy brown hair and softly rounded shoulders. From the front she is a girl with green eyes and large breasts, a body that could stand naked in the street, like a statue, as if it were the example of how a body should look. Hardly talks. I talk too much because she hardly talks.

Ruth submits to sex as to everything else. If she talked, I'd feel more affection and less pity.

Her clothes, the furniture and pictures in her room—she has good taste. Her family is well off. There is a difference between Ruth whose family has money and someone who has good taste but no family money. Nothing in her room bespeaks clever selection, or special discernment, or lucky finds in antique or junk shops. Everything she owns is simply tasteful, expensive, and new.

Feb. 13, '65

"What does your father do?"

"A professor."

"Professor of what?"

"Plant pathology."

"Where?"

"Ohio."

"At what university in Ohio is your father a professor of plant pathology?"

She smiles, suspects I'm teasing her. Shyness is a pathology.

Ruth would help me clean my apartment, if I asked her to. She can't think of it by herself. She's been spoiled by her parents. I clean, but not without the bad dark pleasure of resentment. She watches.

"So you grew up on a farm?" I said, washing dishes and stacking them with excessive care, making a show of it.

"Yes."

"That's nice."

"I don't know."

"You don't? Maybe you should ask somebody."

"I should?"

She isn't an idiot, just very unhappy, so it's difficult for her to think. I don't really care if she helps me clean the apartment or not.

Feb. 14, '65

Harvey can teach himself to play any musical instrument, a fantastic gift, albeit mechanical. He says he can play complicated pieces of music forward or backward.

"If I could play as well as you, I would play much better," I said.

"Did you make that up?"

"Yes."

I read the remark in Italo Svevo. If I said so, I'd have to tell Harvey that Svevo is a great Italian writer. I'd feel pretentious. Better to lie. I will write a book of etiquette for neurotics.

Harvey picks up a newspaper and reads it aloud backward as fast as I can read it forward. I snatch the newspaper away and shout, "Tell me what you read." He says, "Airplane crash. Pilot failed to make a critical adjustment on takeoff. Fifty-eight people killed."

Harvey's hair is a dusty orange-red with dense wiry curls. He must have seen himself in the red Mercedes, but he'd never have bought the car if it actually looked like him. A homely clothes model wouldn't do much for sales. Reality has no appeal. Few people can live with it; therefore, most are more or less crazy. It's possible to imagine that certifiably crazy people in hospitals are sometimes less crazy than those walking the streets.

Harvey knew before he bought the Mercedes that the windshield wipers didn't work, but he figured the car was a good deal. Now he doesn't want to have the windshield wipers repaired. Too expensive. The deal won't seem good.

Harvey built a contraption to move the wipers by tugging a wire drawn through a slightly opened window on the driver's side. He tugs the wire with his left hand and holds the wheel in his right hand. Rain splashes into the Mercedes through the slightly open window and the wipers move slowly. His contraption is ingenious, but in a rainstorm he drives nearly blind, which gives him another reason to be furious with himself.

Feb. 15, '65

I asked Harvey if he knows how to do an abortion. He said, "I'm in medical school. Don't talk to me about abortions. I should leave this minute. Who needs an abortion?"

"Ruth."

"You met her a few days ago," he said. His lips were writhing with evil amusement.

"She was already pregnant."

"Who did it?"

"Some guy who is now in the army."

"Wants to protect his country."

Feb. 16, '65

Harvey said he shits twenty times a day. I'm not surprised. He is a nervous person. He is skinny and stands with a slumped posture, his head thrust forward, and he talks fast in a muttering voice, his small brown eyes darting in every direction as if he were menaced by invisible predators.

Harvey comes to see me to escape loneliness. Has no girl. I'm his only friend. I am also Burt's only friend, but he has a girl. I spend hours with Harvey. He asked me to tell him about literary criticism—what do critics do. I told him that critics look for ambiguity in the words of a poem. Before I could say another word, he said, "What's the point of that? A word is the lowest common denominator of meaning. You want to look for ambiguity, you'll find it. There's hardly anything else. You're supposed to look for meaning. If you say something, you mean something. If it's not in the words, you still mean something. Even if it isn't what the words say, you mean something, or you couldn't say anything except duh, duh, duh."

His remarks were so quick and fierce they shut me up. I was pissed off, but didn't want to argue. If Harvey didn't want me to tell him about literary criticism, he shouldn't have asked. I was still pissed off hours later, thinking about what he said. "A rose is a rose is a rose." This means that a rose is not a word, not ambiguous, and it is not for analysis. It is what it is. Like a part of God, the great "I am that I am."

Harvey dramatizes himself. He makes himself a character, and makes me laugh. But I do it to myself. Walking in the street, I hear someone laughing, then realize it's me. I'd thought of something funny. This is a Jewish trait, not evidence of insanity.

Harvey respects and admires campus athletes, but says that when he sees a big, handsome, healthy, powerfully built football player coming toward him in the street, he wants to leap on the guy's chest and tear his eyes out.

Feb. 17, '65

The landlord is a biologist. As I wheeled my bike out of the house this afternoon, he was returning from his lab. I asked if he knew about bikes and showed him the problem with mine. He kneeled to examine it, saying he doesn't have the time to fix my bike. I didn't ask him to fix it, though maybe I hoped he would offer. Then, to my surprise and distress, I couldn't stop him. He got tools from his apartment and began working grimly on my bike. A highly intelligent Irishman, brooding and angry and strange, doing me a favor I didn't ask for. He said nothing and kept on working until he fixed my bicycle. I mumbled thanks. He walked away, as if he'd fulfilled a nasty obligation. I felt sorry about the incident, but I hadn't asked him to waste his time. As for what made him angry, it wasn't fixing my bike. His apartment is below mine and he sometimes hears me fucking, which makes him feel that his life is narrow and pleasureless. But I didn't tell him to get married and have babies. He has no idea how unhappy I am. If he knew, I'm sure he'd think better of me. That he fixed the bicycle speaks well for the man. It's very decent of him to do it for someone he has reason to dislike—me. I think I'm correct in regard to his feelings. He is a complex moral being who, on another occasion, might as soon kill me as fix my bike.

Harvey is uncoordinated, scrawny, and not strong except in jerky, nervous spasms. Nervous strength; mainly in his fingers. He can't play football, but could be a chess champion if his brain didn't make him feel evil.

Harvey told me about a girl he saw in the library. Spittle sparkled in the corners of his mouth. He said, "She was flawless." He was badly upset by the flawless girl and couldn't sit still in the library and pretend to read. He went to the card file, pulled out a drawer, and in a spasm of fury he mixed up the cards. It was like his desire to tear the eyes out of the handsome football player. Because of the flawless girl, Harvey might blow up the library. The Greeks burned Troy because of Helen. There will be a story in the newspapers, but no poems, alas. I began to ache for the flawless girl, and I said bitterly, "The flawless girl is a B-minus student. If she weren't pretty her grades would be lower."

I said this to make Harvey feel better, but I was thinking she is doubtless a genius and neither Harvey nor I would ever have her.

"True."

"Believe me, B-minus," I said with conviction, though I was already deeply in love with her mind.

"I believe you."

"I see a roomful of engineering majors with skin trouble. They have slide rules sticking out of their shirt pockets. Do I give a shit if they are A students?"

"No."

"But I see one little honey in the back of the room, with only half a brain, and I cheer up."

"Don't stop."

"My feelings are not unique," I said.

"No."

"The library girl should be applauded, but her memory is feeble. She understands little and forgets what she understands. Beyond that, she has nothing to say. She opens and shuts her eyes, no more. Why do you think two thousand guys want to get into her pants?"

"Nature's way of improving the appearance of the race."

"Right. But you, Harvey Baumshlong, get high grades without studying. The flawless girl knows there are such people as Harvey."

"She knows."

"She makes you unhappy? You make her as unhappy, too. It's justice."

"Who wants justice?"

"What do you want?"

"Revenge."

Feb. 19, '65

At the osteopathic clinic in Detroit, Ruth can get an abortion. The clinic is an institution. Women come from everywhere, society matrons, college girls, housewives, hookers. Cops are paid off. The clinic is a factory, five or six women wait in separate booths. The osteopath goes from one to another. A clean, efficient operation in a conservative state. There are nurses, too.

I asked Ruth when was her last period. She gets sullen, as if I asked the wrong question. Doesn't want to think about it. Wants it to go away. Do I want to think about it? Do I want to borrow a car, and then drive her to the clinic in Detroit? I don't want to do anything like that. Neither of us wants it. She's right. Things are best left unquestioned, unexamined, or this wouldn't be happening.

Ruth might have gone home with twenty guys before me. More than twenty. But the number doesn't matter. In my senior year in high school, I made love to a virgin. I was fifteen, a virgin, too. I didn't know what I was doing. She guided me with her hand, drew me into her. She knew where to find herself which made her seem too matter-of-fact for such an intensely spiritual occasion. No wonder abortion is illegal.

The opposite of mystery is pornography.

Feb. 20, '65

Harvey believed that shitting twenty times a day meant he had colon cancer. He went to a doctor who told him he had colitis. Harvey was exhilarated by the great news. He rushed from the doctor's office and stopped people in the street, stangers, and asked them to come to a party at his apartment. The strangers came, and brought other strangers. They drank his beer and stole his medical books. But Harvey met Marie at his party, a girl from Indiana. She gave him her phone number. He is now more or less happy, which is to say anxious in a different way.

Harvey tells me about his impulsiveness as if he were talking about another person. Little tears gleam. But he is in love. He doesn't have his medical books, which cost a fortune, but he has a date with Marie. He goes to secondhand bookstores trying to find his medical books and buy them back.

Harvey's professors hate him, he says, because he is surly and disrespectful and doesn't attend lectures. They would like to have him expelled, but he is the best in his class. He can't be expelled unless he punches a professor or commits a moral turpitude. He has a photographic memory, he says. His tone is spiteful rather than proud. I asked how he will study for exams without his medical books. He says he will borrow lecture notes from other students and memorize them. He needs only one night to memorize months of lectures.

Harvey plays the piano with ferocious fingers, loud as possible, possessed by feelings, but it's nothing in the music he feels. He feels his feelings. He will be a great doctor if forbidden to touch people.

Harvey said the university is right to give scholarships to illiterate, ineducable athletes. "Who needs another history major with a C average?" His question was full of angry righteousness. Why does he care? He is contemptuous of most people and himself. For athletes he feels abject admiration mixed with hate. Girls and animals are uncritically adored. I'm not surprised that he adores girls, but why animals? He must think they are the same as girls.

Feb. 21, '65

Marie is an airline stewardess, often out of town, either in the air or wandering in cities where she doesn't know the language. She loves her job. Her hair is white-blond and straight, cut in bangs. She has large gray, slightly thyroidal, shining eyes in a round white face with a tiny pointed chin. Her face is scarred by acne but not disfigured. It's rather poignant. God will never let her plane crash.

When Harvey does something weird, Marie says, "That's how the Jewish are."

Marie never met a Jew before Harvey. She thinks he is representative, and isn't put off by his numerous peculiarities. He worships Marie, buys her presents, and imagines that he violates her. It is like the relation of primitive people to a god—adoration and violation. Harvey said they were having sex when the telephone rang. He said, "It rang twenty-nine times." He glanced slyly at me to see if I understood how he knew it rang twenty-nine times.

Marie told Harvey that her former boyfriend joined the marines. He came to town, all the way from Indiana, to say goodbye and reminisce about their high-school days. She was nostalgic and lyrical about their goodbye. Harvey asked, "Did you have sex with him?"

Marie said, "No."

"All you did was talk about high school?"

"Not exactly."

Harvey had a fit, screaming at her. "Tell me what you did."

Marie, taken aback, said, "I only went down on him."

Harvey said, "Why did I have to ask?" and then became philosophical. "She's from a farm, doesn't know her value." Harvey is from New York. He knows his value. He and she have a real relationship, and will probably get married. Harvey is afraid to tell his parents that Marie isn't Jewish.

Harvey never laughs. He makes a tight smile; doesn't want to show his teeth. He isn't generous with feelings. Laughing is like giving something away. He is violently expressive or he keeps feelings locked up like money. On such savings, there is negative interest—bitterness. When I laugh Harvey watches with his tight, crooked smile, as if he were envious.

Feb. 22, '65

Harvey never asks how I'm doing, or what's new. He shows up every day and never calls first. Knock, knock. Harvey is at the door. I'm always available since I have nothing to do except read for my qualifying exams. Harvey reads at lightning speed, so he thinks it's the same as doing nothing. He comes in and goes directly to the bathroom. I was reading Dryden's essay on poetry when Harvey arrived and went to the bathroom. I tried to forget his colitis and keep on reading. He came out of the bathroom holding a jar of Vaseline that he found in my medicine cabinet. "I hope this wasn't used for an obscene purpose," he said, lips writhing with repressed mirth.

Feb. 23, '65

I rented a car and drove us to Detroit. Ruth went into the clinic alone. I waited in the car, parked outside the clinic, smoking cigarettes. It was a sunny, cold, brilliant Michigan afternoon—invigorating, and yet you don't want to move. The sunlight calls, the cold forbids. The car was warm. I settled into my coat, and after a while I dozed. Ruth opened the car door about an hour later. I was startled awake, didn't know where I was. She plopped into the seat.

"He won't do it," she sobbed, the words running together.

"Why?"

"Too late."

"He examined you?"

She nodded yes, didn't want to talk, and wouldn't turn her face toward me. She slumped in the seat, staring straight ahead, sullen again. I said, "We'll find someone." I wanted to touch her but she was steeped in her feelings—humiliated, frustrated, angry, untouchable. I drove us back to Ann Arbor. Icy roads. The landscape flat and bleak. She didn't say a word, didn't change her posture. Her silence and depression made me very tense. I was anxious to do something for her, make things O.K. Couldn't abandon her.

I remember I was startled, frightened awake, when the car door opened. I felt a rush of cold air, looked, and saw Ruth bending to enter the car. I saw her twist and drop into the seat. The car shuddered and dipped. It struck me that Ruth is physically substantial. I hadn't realized until that minute that Ruth weighs something definitely. I hadn't felt it, or taken it in, the realization that she is large-boned, large-breasted, a full-grown woman, a physical being who exists independently of my feelings. It doesn't matter if I think she is a handsome country girl, or that her hair is a beautiful chestnut brown. My feelings and thoughts are mine, and have nothing to do with what she is. By the same token, her trouble is hers, inherent in her substantial body. Her trouble is not mine. I didn't actually know this, didn't realize it, until the car dipped and shuddered beneath her weight.

There is an absolute disconnection between you and anyone else; also between you and yourself. I want to believe that for some reason, but in the morgue, when they presented her and I looked at Sylvia, I fell backward as if I'd been punched in the face. They didn't ask me, after that happened, to identify her.

Feb. 24, '65

Ruth is usually passive and silent, yet she has the irascible moods of a spoiled child. I sometimes think she is angry at me, as if I should give her more or do more for her, but I don't know what she thinks. It must be that I think I owe her more. I resent the idea of owing her anything at all.

I phoned Karen, who knows lefty politicos. Parsons, her boyfriend, deals marijuana. They know everyone political or shady. Karen said it might take a little time to find a doctor, but she was confident and encouraging. I was much relieved, as if she'd assumed responsibility for Ruth. I feel a huge sense of gratitude to Karen. I am no longer alone.

Feb. 25, '65

Karen heard about a doctor in East Lansing. I said we'll go to him. She said you can't go to him. He doesn't want to be identified. If he agrees to do it, he'll come to Ann Arbor. I said I'll call him. She said you can't call him. She will call him. Then we have to wait for him to call us. We must be ready, at a moment's notice, whenever he can do it.

I told Ruth about the doctor. She was in a deep, deep sulk and didn't respond. It's as if nothing makes any difference anymore. I said people are trying to help. Don't make things harder. She mumbled a word. It wasn't "Thanks."

Ruth has never said "Thanks." Her expression is like bad weather. She sits for hours, in her apartment or mine, staring at nothing. If she's angry at me, I don't know why. Maybe she doesn't really want a doctor. Maybe she wants to marry me and play house. Now I'm angry at her.

Harvey came by. He wouldn't talk to me with Ruth in the apartment. I had to go out in the hall. He whispered, "Do you know what would happen to me if the medical school found out I was involved?" I told him he isn't involved. He asked if I had a lead on a doctor. I told him Karen knew someone. "I don't want to hear about it," he said, then asked who Karen knew.

"A doctor."

"A real doctor?"

"Yes."

"Don't tell me his name."

"I don't know his name."

"Have a pair of pliers ready."

"What for?"

"The umbilical cord."

I thought he was joking. He wasn't joking.

Feb. 27, '65

Harvey went home to the Bronx to tell his parents about Marie, and came right back. His father told him there was no place for Harvey to put his suitcase. "Under my bed," Harvey said, but his father didn't want the suitcase under any bed, or in a closet, or in the garage. He said he can't sleep if there is a suitcase in the house. Harvey put his suitcase outside, hidden in the bushes.

"In the bushes," he said, watching my face, waiting for me to laugh. I wanted to cry.

He told his father about Marie. His father said, "Let's discuss this calmly." Then he jumped onto a couch, waving his arms and shrieking about Harvey's intention to marry a girl who isn't Jewish. Harvey waited to hear what I made of that, but I didn't have anything to say. I imagined his father on the couch, waving his arms and shrieking. Harvey didn't seem upset or displeased or even mystified by his father's reaction. He'd been dreading it and is glad it's over.

Ruth and I fell asleep waiting for the doctor to call. I was worried that someone else would call and the line would be busy. Nobody called. Among my friends who know what's going on are Karen, Parsons, Harvey, Kerry, Wood, Burt, and Goldie. I don't know how many of Karen's friends know. I don't know how many have told other people. I think plenty of people know, maybe half the student population, about thirteen thousand students. There's also Ruth's friends, but she hasn't seen anyone except me and the osteopath. She doesn't talk, anyway.

Feb. 28, '65

The doctor called. Ruth talked to him briefly, and then she was utterly changed, gleeful, childlike, happy for the first time since I met her. In her mind it's virtually finished because a doctor talked to her on the phone. She's foolish. It isn't finished. There is plenty still to worry about.

Ruth said the doctor will call again tomorrow night, then come to my apartment. He wants me to be here, but I mustn't see him. I am to stay in the bathroom, the door shut, and remain with Ruth when he leaves. Must be no lights on in the apartment. His fee is seventy-five dollars. Karen said he does abortions as a service to women, and charges only for his expenses. She didn't tell me his name. She said only that he was black, and he was from a town near East Lansing.

"What kind of doctor?"

"A specialist, a big shot. No more questions."

Ruth didn't ask questions. She went to the bank and withdrew seventy-five dollars.

March 1, '65

The doctor called at eight o'clock and said he'd be here in twenty minutes. We shut the lights, as we'd been told to do, and then sat on the couch in the living room. The couch was opened into a bed, made up with clean sheets. When the doctor knocked I went into the bathroom and shut the door. I heard Ruth open the door and heard murmuring, but no words. It seemed only about fifteen minutes passed, and then Ruth called me. I came out of the bathroom and turned on a light. I hadn't heard the doctor leave. Ruth was sitting up in the bed, fully clothed. She said he'd used forceps. It was done. Done quickly in the dark, but she said part was still inside her. The doctor told her it would come out by itself. He'd taken the other part with him, and left a bottle of antibiotics. I was appalled, and unable to speak for fear of upsetting her. Besides, it was done. In part.

Ruth seemed merely a little put out, and went into the bathroom and sat there. I asked several times, "Anything happening?" She said each time, "No." Her favorite word. I hadn't expected anything like this. I was scared out of my mind. She was being sullen again. I said, "Let's go to Karen's place." I didn't want to be alone with Ruth. I needed people who talked. "Do you feel all right?" I asked. She shrugged. She didn't object to walking across town. Didn't say anything. We met a few weeks ago. It feels like years. I don't even know her. She has freckles, a wholesome pretty face, a substantial big-boned body, and the moods of a spoiled kid. So what? It tells me nothing. This is about action.

At Karen's place, Ruth went straight into the bathroom. She sat on the bowl, elbows on her knees, head in her hands, and didn't shut the door. Karen and Parsons talked to her. Then Harvey arrived, his red hair exuding hysteria. He didn't want to be here, and couldn't keep away. He stood in the bathroom door and looked. Ruth pushed the door shut. He made her self-conscious. Her legs were totally exposed. They are nice legs. She felt prurience in Harvey's looking. Marie arrived after Harvey. She looked dopey and happy, still feeling the thrill of her last flight. "Where have you been, Marie?" She said, "Cleveland," and rolled her eyes and laughed, as if she'd said something funny. She laughs at almost everything she says—"It's my birthday, ha, ha." "I bought a new dress, ha, ha,"—and people laugh with her. They don't know what's supposed to be funny, but she makes everyone as dopey as herself. That's her charm and Harvey adores her. He's a genius, but Marie is his light, his only happiness.

About three hours passed with Ruth sitting in the bathroom. The rest of us played cards. Karen gave us beers. The boys went outside to piss. Karen didn't seem to feel any need. Nobody paid attention to Ruth. People came by and left, friends of Karen and Parsons. I knew none of them except for the agitator who makes speeches on campus. He has a smooth tenor voice, and is very earnest about political issues. Every week he has another issue. His tenor voice is sort of female in sincerity and earnestness, very musical, as if he is crooning when he talks about social injustice and the evil of American foreign policy. To him political issues have a sensual value. He talks politics the way Chet Baker sings about love, but he hasn't Baker's talent, only the tenor, the female quality. Harvey says, "He puts down America, the best country in the history of the world. So fuck him." That's one difference between us. I have an impractical aesthetic mind. His mind is a butcher knife.

When the agitator left, Karen said he had asked her to have sex with him. She was upset. She slapped the wall with a dish towel.

He'd told her that he'd been very busy, and needed the release. Would she accommodate? Karen had admired him, been proud to be his friend. He was courageous, unashamed of speaking in public. She now felt he had no respect for her. I was surprised at her vehemence. My leftie friends always treated women that way, like equals. Parsons grinned all about at the people in the room. His posture was stiff. He stopped grinning. His face went flat, and then he grinned again and went flat again, as if an electric charge shot through his jaw intermittently. He was uncomfortable, restless, shaken by the event and Karen's distress. He felt an allegiance to the agitator, but Karen was his girl. After a while, Parsons resolved his doubt. He said, "I'll kill the cocksucker."

"You won't do anything," said Karen.

Parsons would kill the agitator. Parsons is a berserker. I saw him in a fistfight at a party. He was fearless, snarling with hate rather than anger. A middle-class white boy from Dearborn against three black Uhuru kids who'd crashed the party and beaten up the host, also black, for no reason. Parsons' cold eyes and a hard weird grin, like a rictus. Karen, a sweet Jewish girl from Brooklyn, motherly, has high social ideals and believes she can make the world better.

People came and went, as if there were a kind of loose party in progress. They made a little conversation, drank a beer, glanced toward the bathroom, the door now shut, and then left. There was nothing to see. It was a boring event. Kerry and Wood showed up near midnight. Kerry light, and Wood very black. He looks like African royalty, a slender prince with a wide flat chest and broad shoulders. "What's happening?" asked Kerry. I told him. He made no comment and asked no more questions. Wood said nothing. Nobody talked about what was happening in the bathroom. Hours passed. Boys went outside to piss. None of the girls left to piss—not that I'd noticed. They must have.

Harvey asked Karen if she had pliers. "What for?" she said. He muttered unintelligibly. He wanted to contribute, give his expert help, but couldn't speak clearly. The medical school might hear what he said. His career would be over, etc.

Parsons said, "You're in med school. When it comes out, man, you take over. Carry it to the Huron River and throw it in. The water will tear it to pieces." He laughed like a lunatic. Maybe he was still thinking of the agitator.

"They teach you that in med school?" said Wood, low and serious, with a black Texas accent. "I wouldn't go near the river at home. Too many cottonmouths." Wood is very funny, but you have to know him to know when he's joking. Harvey suspected a joke and smiled, but looked as if he might vomit.

Ruth whimpered.

We all went to the bathroom and crowded at the door. Ruth was standing, holding her skirt high up on her long legs, and looking into the bowl. I saw it.

Eyes were bluish bulges. The hands appeared completely formed, much like Ruth's, with long fingers, finely shaped. The hands were heartbreaking. What do you do with your feelings? I'd thought only of Ruth until then. The body ended halfway down. No bottom, no sex.

"What did the doctor look like?"

Ruth said, "I don't know."

He was black and did the whole thing in the dark, but she must have seen him for an instant in the hall light when she opened the door. He was God, as far as she was concerned. Invisible. I imagined a small man, but he might have been big. He was strong, absolutely for sure, a grip of steel.

Harvey pressed by me, looked. No umbilical cord—gone with the sex and the legs. Harvey had nothing to contribute and took Marie's arm and pulled her after him toward the door. She didn't want to leave. He prevailed, pulling her out the door. This wasn't a good place to be, but I couldn't leave.

Ruth emerged from the bathroom for the first time that night. Parsons reached into the bowl, and using both hands lifted it out and carried it into the kitchen, and then wrapped it in paper towels and set it on the counter. He was caught up in the momentum of things, on stage. It was his moment, but he moved quickly to get it over with, and then turned his back on it, leaving it on the counter wrapped in paper towels. We all went into the living room. Ruth lay on the couch. Karen covered her with a blanket. Nobody felt too good, or had much to say. I supposed we were all complicit. Only Harvey had fled, but he had the most to lose, presumably. Parsons now became our leader, loud and matter-of-fact, as if showing off his cool. "Too early to go to the river, too many cars. We'll go after midnight."

Karen shouted, "Oh God, oh God."

Her cat was on the counter, clawing at the paper towels to get at the contents. Karen ran to the counter and slapped the cat. It was avid, hissing, wouldn't retreat. Parsons picked up a beer bottle and strode into the kitchen. He'd have brained the cat, but it saw him coming and leaped off the counter. A cat can tell Parsons is dangerous.

Karen said to Parsons, "Go away. I'll take care of it." She picked up the cat and carried it outside, then returned. She rewrapped the body and put it into the refrigerator.

After a while Parsons said, "Let's go. Ruth, get off your ass. Let's go." He didn't want to wait. He was high and wild.

Ruth said, "I would like to bury it in the country."

Kerry said gently. "We'll go with Parsons, then drive you home, Ruth."

She got off the couch, obedient as always. Nobody paid attention to what she'd said.

I went in Kerry's car with Ruth and Wood. Parsons carried the thing and rode in Karen's car. Kerry followed Karen's car to the bridge. Both cars turned off their headlights. Parsons got out and stood for a moment in the moonlight and wind. We had a good look at him. Then he threw it off the bridge. The package came apart. White paper fluttered in the moonlight, then vanished. There was no sound except the wind.

Driving to Ruth's place Kerry stopped at the side of the road, got out of the car, and took a long piss. We watched until he finished. It was outrageous. Ruth sat there watching, expressionless. She'd been on exhibit half the night sitting on the toilet bowl. Kerry taking a piss meant ordinary life had resumed. I glanced at Wood to see what he made of it. His eyes moved, met mine, that's all. A master of opacity. If I didn't know him well, I'd not have realized he was getting a kick out of Kerry pissing. I got a kick out of Wood getting a kick out of it.

At Ruth's place, Kerry said, "She'll be all right. Stay with us, man." I wanted to stay, but I got out of the car. "I have to stay with her," I said. "Doctor's orders."

Ruth slept hard, breathing through her mouth. I turned on the lamp beside her desk. She had a new Olivetti typewriter, a pile of art books, a gold pocket watch, silver bracelets, rings and other jewelry. Clothing was strewn around the room. Her parents adore her. It was almost dawn. I watched her sleep. She looked angelic. I lay down beside her. Her breath was sweet, too.

March 2, '65

The Student Union cafeteria. Goldie was sitting by herself. People were at tables all around. I walked quickly among the tables to her table, and was extremely self-conscious, as if everybody knew something terrible about me. I focused on Goldie, and cut off peripheral vision. If I didn't see them, they didn't see me. Goldie watched my approach. When I reached her table, I sat down quickly, and then I felt safe. She made her snort-laugh, then laughed openly in a friendly kind of pitying style. She'd heard the story, and had formed an opinion of me.

She said, "They'll eat you alive."

"Who?"

She snorted again and looked at the tabletop.

I asked again, "Who?"

Her small calm knowing smile and silence. Dark, self-assured, suburban Detroit girl with long finely shaped fingers and aquiline, biblical face. She said, "People," as though it was obvious, and I'd made her impatient.

 *When I first came to Michigan, in the mid-fifties, I had no teaching job. I supported myself by writing papers for undergraduates, and working in a pharmacology lab. It was nightmarish work. A study of morphine addiction in monkeys was under way. The monkeys were caged in a basement, dismal as a dungeon. They would huddle in corners and shriek at me and bare their teeth in a nasty grin. My job was to clean the cages with a hose. I'd open a cage door and a monkey would come flying out, and then I'd enter the cage and shoot water all about, sending the monkey's excretions and various debris down a drain. When I finished, I stepped away from the door and the monkey would fly back into the cage. I was fond of the monkeys, but they weren't fond of me and they hated the people who injected them with morphine. After a while their hideous little shrieking faces became almost unbearable. I felt pity mixed with disgust. The fear and neediness in their eyes asked too much of me. They asked to be released from the horror of morphine, which made their own bodies a cage. Once,*

the monkeys escaped and went flying around the campus. Nobody both-
ered to recapture them. They returned for their morphine shot, abject and
terrified, badly strung out, scrambling back into their cages. People were
so amused. Scrawny, little, hysterical, addicted monkeys.

My roommate, Taylor North, who got me the job cleaning cages, was
a Ph.D. candidate in philosophy, specializing in mathematical logic.
He'd soon be hired, at a high salary, by the computer industry. Taylor's
job was to inject the monkeys. He'd open a cage door and a monkey
would come out instantly, sometimes vaulting off Taylor's head, and go
zipping about the dungeon. Taylor waited until the monkey settled out-
side its own cage, clinging to the bars and presenting its back to the nee-
dle. Trembling and squealing, the monkey looked down over its shoulder
with dread, watching Taylor approach. Taylor reached up with one hand,
clasped the monkey's lower back, and then injected the monkey with the
other hand. One night as morphine flowed into the trembling monkey,
the animal shit in Taylor's face.

After the monkeys, I got a job as a teaching assistant. The professor
I assisted was Austin Warren, an important name in literary scholarship
and criticism, and a charismatic teacher. For years afterward I had one or
another kind of teaching job in the following states: Michigan, New Jer-
sey, California, Iowa, New York, Maryland, Alabama, and Colorado.

Sometime in late March 1965, I met Priscilla Older and a few
weeks later she was pregnant and we got married. This period isn't
much noticed in my journal. I was studying day and night for my doc-
toral exams. Priscilla helped by reading authors I found unbearable and
marking crucial passages.

April 10, '65
I wanted to write a story about the time Ernie bought a twelve-
gauge shotgun. "Someone knocks when I'm not home, don't open
the door," he said. He had a gambling debt and didn't want to pay,

though he could pay. If he hadn't been so theatrical, I'd have believed he was in a dangerous situation. Ernie stacked couch pillows at the end of the hall and fired at them. The noise was loud and stunning. Thud-stunning. Wherever that shell hit you—a leg, an arm—the sheer impact would break bones and send devastating vibrations through your body and kill you. Ernie was trembling afterward, and went strutting about the apartment as if he'd confronted the gamblers and taught them a lesson. He looked at me furtively, a cowardly sneering smile in his fat mouth. There was a big hole where the shot passed through all three pillows and entered the wall. He'd frightened himself. When the gamblers phoned and told him they were coming by for their money, Ernie phoned the police and said there were four black guys in a red Cadillac coming up State Street with guns in the trunk. The police stopped the Cadillac and searched it. They didn't find guns, but the gamblers turned around and went back to Detroit, and Ernie packed and went back to Chicago where he made his crooked investment in the stock market, lost a fortune, and was in great debt to the mob. He could have paid the debt somehow, but chose to kill himself. The story failed.

Nov. 25, '65
I won the fiction award of the *Massachusetts Review* judged by Philip Roth. My first thought was, "Did he remember that we'd met at Bill Cole's apartment, and later spent an evening together, he and his wife, and me and Eleanor Klein?" I'll use the money to pay my phone bill. My cough is three months old. I wanted to go to New York for Thanksgiving, but I'm coughing and it's a twelve-hour drive.

Dec. 29, '65
Priscilla was in labor approximately forty-eight hours. Dr. Work was in and out of the room with nothing to say. I stopped him in the

hall and told him she was in a lot of pain. He said, "Pain never killed anybody," and he went on by. He didn't know why her labor took so long, and had her X-rayed. Everything was normal. I phoned Mel Seltzer and asked him to come to the hospital and introduce himself to Dr. Work, who would then maybe tell another doctor what he was unwilling to tell me. Dr. Work told Mel there was nothing wrong with Priscilla or the baby. He was just as mystified as everyone else about why it was taking so long. I wanted my baby and I was going crazy. Then Ethan arrived.

Dec. 30, '65

I have a wife and a baby. My friends are Michael Katz, Peter Steinberger, Jean Tenander, Burt Welcher, Penny Carnahan, Tony Friedman, Mel Seltzer, Terry Ray, Durward Collins, Tony Drago, Bob and Paula Stern. In California there are Allen Bergson, Julie Rountree, Fred Amory, Sue Coleman, and Julian and Zelda Boyd. Naomi Kane, Malcolm Raphael, Stanley Moskowitz, Bernie Kendler, Steve Shrader, and others are in New York. Priscilla's friends are in Cleveland. I don't know of any in Ann Arbor.

 *In 1966 I published stories, began writing a dissertation on the poetry of Byron, and bought my first car, a Saab station wagon. We drove to California with our son, Ethan, who wasn't yet walking, and our black dog, Byron, a Lab-setter mix. I'd been hired by the English department of the University of California at Davis. People in the Berkeley English department, where I'd been a graduate student from 1958–60, would invite us to parties. We drove down from Davis, about sixty miles northeast of Berkeley. I wanted to be hired by Berkeley, but always praised Davis, saying I liked the town*

and the department. True enough, but I thought Berkeley was the best place in America to live and work. Through the influence of the eminent, elegant, and adorable Mark Schorer, I was invited to visit the Berkeley English department for one quarter and then was offered a job. According to gossip, my appointment was supported by the people I liked, and opposed by a man who was one of the reasons I quit graduate school years earlier. It seemed there were too many nitwits like him in English, but now I had a family, and no other way to make a living, and I wanted the best job I could get. At the time, despite the nitwit, Berkeley had the best department in the country. A difference between Berkeley and Davis was in departmental conversation. It tended to be normal and friendly at Davis until a political issue arose and then there might be shouting in the halls and slammed doors. At Berkeley nothing was normal, but everybody was invincibly polite and there were more laughs.

May 1, '67
Berkeley party:

    "So you're Deirdre."

    "That's an uneducated pronunciation of my name."

    "Have you studied Celtic?"

    "That's an uneducated pronunciation of 'Celtic.'"

    "In the history of the language . . ."

    "I'm not interested in technicalities."

"I'm Maka. I don't think we've been introduced."

    "Do you know what Maka means in Japanese?"

    "Tell me."

    "Squat, ugly toad."

"I'm so glad you came to the party."

    "Do you know what your name means?"

"My name?"

"It's Foster, isn't it?"

"Cassandra Foster."

"I don't care about Foster. That's the family. It belongs to thousands of people."

"What about Cassandra?"

"Cassandra means wretched old hag."

"Tell me when you stopped loving your children."

"I wish he'd take the job at Harvard and leave Berkeley. Both universities would be better off."

"I heard Jim went backpacking."

"I know whose back he's packing."

"But he's married."

"So are all the gay men in the department."

"She wrote an impressive book on transcendentalism."

"She's my girlfriend."

"You're kidding. You don't mean it."

"Yes, yes. I finger her while she's on the phone talking to her husband."

"If you hire a second-rater, he'll hire a third-rater. This is the lame-o principle of English departments going downhill. Only the first rate hire the first rate."

"He went to British public schools. He had no idea that he was straight until he was over fifty years old and came to Berkeley."

June 1, '67

I asked if she'd been unfaithful to me. Priscilla said, "Do you think I'm an animal?" If she'd said, "No," I wouldn't have needed a cigarette.

June 10, '69

Possible story: A relative visits for an indefinite stay. Signs of his presence appear all over the house, his pipe in an ashtray, his newspaper in the bathroom. He practices the violin several hours a day, and invites a girlfriend to dinner. She sometimes stays overnight, and then she moves in with him. The host won't say anything but he is angry, so he denies himself comforts—won't smoke, eat, read, sleep, or talk. This is to suggest to the relative how the host feels, and to suggest that the host wants the relative to go away. The relative notices but doesn't understand. He responds by fixing things about the house, calling attention to neglect the house has suffered. He rewires the basement, repairs the broken concrete sidewalk, and offers to paint the living room. Finally, the host blows up and they have an angry exchange. The relative, much offended, packs and leaves with his girlfriend. The host, further outraged, runs after them in the street, demanding that they return immediately.

June 30, '69

Invited to Notre Dame for literary festival with Tom Stoppard, Richard Gilman, and others. I watched a football practice. The coaches were screaming at the players constantly. Screaming at the defensive backfield: "Honor the fake." "I can see grass." Screaming at the quarterback: "Hurry the pivot, not the pass." Coaches screamed at the offense and defense even as the play was in progress. Several coaches were screaming at once: "Be a hitter." "Don't let him cross." "Don't use your hands when the ball is in the air." "Know where you are on the field." Tom Stoppard was at the practice, too. He said in a hoarse voice, "I wish I hadn't agreed to sing at the faculty club tonight." It was hard not to laugh. I laughed, but I didn't want to because the practice was extremely serious and it seemed disrespectful to laugh. The speed, the violence, the old men screaming at the kids, bodies getting smashed all over the field. At one end of the field you can see a mosaic picture, on the face of a building, of Jesus with his arms raised, as if signaling a touchdown. The seriousness of anything seems like the seriousness of anything else.

Possible story: Professor X discovers a plagiarized paper in his class. It was written by a student he is fond of. She likes the class so much that she once brought her husband to meet the professor and hear his lecture. But now the professor feels betrayed. He doesn't look forward to the confrontation. The idea of it angers him. At the confrontation he tells her that he showed her paper to a colleague who recognized it as having been submitted to him in a course he taught a year ago. The girl confesses that the paper had been submitted to the other professor by her husband. But she had written it for him. Her husband insisted that she get credit for her work so she resubmitted it this year to Professor X. She knows she did wrong, but it was her paper. She wrote it. She could have written another, but it wouldn't have been as good. She does good work only if it's for someone else. All rewards that might come to her for the work she's done mean nothing to her. Professor X listens without sympathy. He still feels personally betrayed. She says, "I did write the paper. Not for you, but I wrote it." He'd not have thought she could write a paper that good, but even if she did— and he wants to believe her—it doesn't change the way he feels.

Doctor at party last night tells about a girl who played the cello, and his disappointment and fury at meeting her boyfriend, a revolting hippie type, because the girl had symptoms of gonorrhea. The doctor did a throat culture to see if she had it there, too. She did, which meant she'd performed fellatio on the revolting boy. He said his colleagues were aghast when he told them. One of them said, "I suppose young people do such things these days." Quite a few men and women at the party had done a lot more than fellatio, and some had had diseases more exotic than gonorrhea, but the doctor went on about the cellist without the least suspicion that anything had changed since his day when young people didn't "do such things."

Style is the way an action continues to be *like* itself. It's an imitation of necessity. Max J. Friedlander, my favorite art historian, says "unconscious action leads to style. Conscious action to mannerism. . . . the art form, insofar as it springs from the soul, is style, insofar as it issues from the mind is manner."

What you feel in a playground swing, returning from its highest point, falling backward into the belly of its arc, is similar to what you feel trudging up a beach against the tide as it pulls the sand from beneath your feet and each step seems to lose more ground than the last.

Jesse was born in 1969 in San Francisco. We were living in Berkeley in a house on Josephine Street. From early on he was good-looking and wild. Ethan, three years older, complaining about three-year-old Jesse, said, "He's not even tame."

June 10, '72

Jesse said "shit" in front of my mother. She was surprised. He said it again in front of my mother-in-law. She was shocked, then enraged and said, "Innocence corrupted." She wouldn't visit her neighbors with "the child" lest he say "shit" in front of them. She lives in dread of the moment when he will come out with the word.

Naomi came to dinner. We talked about the war. She defends the massacre in southeast Asia because it led to the realization of a Marxist society. She has nothing comparable to fear for herself, though she's been raped, and it's true that she puts herself on the line in America—giving to the "community," organizing, lecturing—and thinks of herself as a servant of the people. Still, it seems gruesome to defend a massacre. With anyone else I'd have started an argument. Naomi is fragile, bright, graceful in all her movements, good-natured, generous, and amusing in her slangy streetwise style when she talks politics or tells stories. She is also a great dancer. When she comes to dinner, I feel happy, and see her politics as a feature of her personality, like her heavy smoking and endless need for coffee. If I didn't like her so much, I wouldn't like her at all.

Possible story: Flora goes to the doctor, but she can't make him agree that she has a pain in her leg. She goes to him again and again with the same complaint. At last he agrees. He says she was right from the beginning, and she needs surgery. She is gratified and frightened. She wanted to hear him say that her condition was grim, but she is very reluctant to have surgery. She decides to try to cure herself with a certain diet. It works. She can hardly wait to return to the doctor. "Him and his surgery, his knife," she says. Her indignation is immense. She seems to have no idea of her good fortune in being treated by such an excellent doctor, but she must know that he frightened her into health. She denounces him every chance she gets and continues to see him year after year.

The Couple. They have arguments in public about political matters, particularly Israel—he's pro, she's against. He says there are political situations about which she might care more, but no, she says this is the most important one. Why? She can't tell him. It seems too obvious to discuss. She is obsessed with Israel. As if making a concession, he says, "The national personality is aggressive." She says, "Obnoxious." He says, "The ideals of liberal democracy have been realized." She says, "There is repression everywhere." He says, "Women have equal rights." She says, "They're treated like shit." Finally, to end the exchange, he says, "All right, the country is founded on an illusion." She says, "It's here, it exists." He doesn't understand her and he often wonders if she would feel deprived of the pleasure she takes in her passionately righteous animosity if Israel vanished. They argue about almost everything else, too. He thinks people have unique talents and intellectual and physical qualities. She says everyone is the same. He says, "Everyone is the same? Would you have married me if I were a midget?" She stares, says nothing, but her look tells him that his question is detestable. She says, "Yes." Then she starts to leave. He says, "Where are you going?" She calls back, "I'm going for a walk in Tilden Park." He slumps, says nothing. It's after midnight. To say the least, it's dangerous for a woman to walk around alone in Tilden Park, but he dare not say the least. She'd have a tantrum, accuse him of restricting her freedom. Nobody tells her where to walk or not walk. Politics, he thinks, is destroying his marriage.

Possible story: Ginger works as a secretary for a journalist on Christopher Street. She says he has a snake head and a big body, so he looks like a dinosaur, and he wears fat smelly tweeds. She edits his manuscripts and makes notes in the margins, little suggestions for improving a sentence or changing a word, but that only takes a few minutes now and then. He doesn't care if she isn't doing anything but sitting in the room and waiting for pages. Mainly he just wants her there all day while he types. He wants her nearby in the small living room of his apartment, his office, with its large oak desk and hissing radiator and million books. So she sits there watching him, and occasionally looks at pages, and the day grows longer, and he forgets that she is in the room, and he begins to scratch himself indecently or to pick his nose, and Ginger says she loves it. The more self-absorbed he becomes, the more disgusting, the more he sinks into the obliviousness of his body, in the heavy smelly tweeds, the more Ginger wants it to continue. She says this not laughing at herself. She says she finds herself "dizzy with the pleasure of it." He's like an animal in the zoo, not conscious of her eyes.

July 30, '72

Naomi was raped for the second time. It happened in her bedroom. The man climbed through the window in the middle of the night. She said she recognized him—somebody she'd seen at work—but couldn't be absolutely sure. People came and went all the time. Apparently, he'd followed her home. She didn't know his name. He climbed in the window and stood at the foot of the bed and undressed, taking off his jacket and shirt and hanging them on the back of a chair. Then he took off the rest of his clothing, and raped her. I heard icy revulsion in Naomi's voice, but no moral comment. Her expression was flat. There was nothing in her eyes except perhaps the memory. For political reasons she won't go to the police. What impressed her, judging by her story, is that he hung his jacket and shirt on the back of a chair. She seems haunted by his deliberateness, and sees it again and again, unable to understand what it means.

May 11, '74

I was sitting at the poolside with Julian. The sun was hot and bright, flashing off the surface of the water, making it hard to follow Julian's argument, which had to do with what he called the Theory of Action. I have no gift for academic philosophy, and the sun was too bright to think. I wanted to ask Julian what the Theory of Action says about people in a hypnotic trance, but feared the question would reveal that I understood nothing. Jesse, fifteen feet away, was in the middle of the flashing pool, flailing at the water, apparently swimming. Suddenly I realized he was going under, not swimming. I jumped into the pool in my clothes and dragged him out.

Neither Julian nor I noticed at first that Jesse was drowning, though it was happening right before our eyes. He's six years old and believes he can do anything, whether he can or not. He'd never cry out for help but keep flailing to the bottom of the pool, believing he was swimming. As for the Theory of Action—my body came out of the chair and jumped into the pool. An action happened. I didn't intend it. I acted. It happened.

It's torture to imagine Jesse out of my sight amid unimaginable dangers. The unthinking, animal intelligence of the body—love?—is of no practical value if you're not around. I didn't feel love as I went flying out of the chair, only a force. There was no me, only it.

Sept. 3, '75

Eating alone—separated from family—feels animalistic and sad. Company civilizes the act, makes you forget, even makes you cheery. I eat standing at the sink. Camus's "stranger" does something like that. I live alone, but there hasn't really been any essential change for me. We always were Mr. Oil and Mrs. Water. In the same bed or in different parts of the country makes no difference.

You have to be rich to know exactly what you look like. For example, my clothes are always an inexact fit. I buy suits off the rack, untailored. Shirts, pants, and shoes are approximations. If I were rich I'd know the precise measurements of my body, and wouldn't dress in conformity to an average size convenient to clothing manufacturers. I'd have shoes made to order because my feet are different sizes. The asymmetry indicates an unreconciled difference between my parents. You see unreconciled differences in almost all faces. There is a major and minor face; for example, blue eyes consorting with a nose that belongs to brown eyes. One face is haunted by another. The dominant face is the more physical. The spiritual face crouches behind it, yearning for the light. No face looks exactly the same from day to day. Whatever you are, you aren't quite.

Dec. 19, '75
All morning I graded final exams. Then went out and played basketball by myself. A chubby woman with a child came up. The woman asked if she could play, too. She wore jeans and sandals, and had a mellow Berkeley manner. I said no. An amazingly rude and ungenerous response. To soften it I said I'm leaving in a minute. I left in half a minute, feeling troubled. Maybe I snapped at her because I was fantasizing as I took shots and dribbled, seeing myself as a sixteen-year-old, quicker than I am, stronger, more graceful; or maybe I was bitter about my divorce, and the woman looked moronically blissful. She was stoned in the middle of the day. With a little kid.

I picked up Ethan and Jesse. Took Ethan to the allergist, then shopped—bread, milk, window-cleaning ammonia, and paint remover for the bedroom dresser—then bought Jesse a twenty-dollar skateboard, then back to the house, then cooked dinner for them, steak with canned green beans, baked potato, and salad. I had coffee later and the kids played with their books and drew pictures. Ethan painted a burning farm and a burning skyscraper. When I started sweeping the kitchen floor, Ethan said, "You're practically famous, and you're sweeping the floor." He looked at me with weary incomprehension.

I remembered a moment, years ago, when I looked into the bathroom—because Jesse had been in there for about a half an hour—and when I opened the door I saw—just as he was leaving—the water rising in the bowl, beginning to flow over the rim. I stopped the flow, but some of it was already on the floor. I spent an hour with a sponge, sopping it up, and then used cleanser on the floor, the side of the bathtub and bowl—shit everywhere. I put bath rugs in the washing machine. Later, testing the toilet, it overflowed again, and again I cleaned up. It didn't seem as horribly offensive the second time. I remembered my panic at the sight of Jesse walking away with the brown water rising behind him. I remember that I accused Jesse of causing the overflow in the toilet by throwing a small toy into the bowl. He said, "Just because I did it before doesn't mean I did it now." I was amused because that sounded like the skeptic's argument. His mother said I was too much his buddy. A father would keep the proper emotional distance.

Nov. 15, '76

Memory: At an auction in Spoonhandle, Alabama, I saw a woman with black hair and eyes who looked very much like another woman—someone with black hair and eyes I couldn't remember. The woman at the auction, who was quite slender, usurped the place of the other woman in my memory, who was also slender, and I kept asking myself, "Who does that woman look like?" I followed her up and down the aisles of furniture and various junk in the huge barn, and the more I looked at her the more she reminded me of the woman, a very particular woman I couldn't remember. The woman at the auction was actually more than slender, actually rather skinny, and had a sickly white complexion, but, as if she were pretending to greater life than she had, she was heavily and brightly bejeweled. When I got up close, I could smell her. She was also heavily perfumed. There seemed to be an artsy quality in her manner. She was fragile, her shoulders thin and sharp and bent as if starting to close toward each other. Her neck was long and slender. I followed her around the huge barn trying to remember and then finally gave up, and went home frustrated by not being able to say who it is she resembled.

When I came home I drew her face from memory. Even before I finished drawing it, I had two thoughts, the second coming almost instantly, almost with the first. I thought of Sylvia, and then Naomi. The woman looked a bit like Sylvia, but much more like Naomi, so much like Naomi it was chilling. The woman at the auction had reminded me of Naomi, but neither she nor Sylvia would come to mind, I think, because they're dead. Somehow looking vaguely alike and being dead they canceled each other. If one started coming up the other canceled it. Meanwhile the living woman was canceling both of them, torturing me with frustration. When I drew her face in my journal and recognized the woman as Naomi, I was thrilled with relief and fear, as if Naomi had come back to life or had never died but merely gone to Alabama to live in hiding. I felt like crying. I'd always liked her so much.

She never took good care of herself and died of a metabolic disorder. She'd stored her things in our garage, including a mass of handwritten political theorizing, testifying to her seriousness, intellectual grandiosity, loneliness. She felt abandoned by comrades who quit "The Movement" to enter "The System," becoming professors and politicians. I did only the usual things—marched against the House Un-American Committee in the late fifties, then against the war, wrote checks to support the good causes, was concerned about environmental issues, etc.

In 1977 I lived in upstate New York, in Tivoli, next door to Bard College, where I taught for a semester. In December, I drove back to California alone.

Christmas Day, '77

I spent Christmas Day on the road in Alabama, Mississippi, and Louisiana, listening to black and white revivalists on the radio. Millions upon millions of pine trees in Alabama and Mississippi on either side of Route 59, a wall of pines. The sun was flickering violently through the pines as I drove south. It was a warm day, about fifty degrees. America was beautiful and not interesting. I stopped in Baton Rouge at a Holiday Inn. A man came up to me and said, "Hey. You see good? Read this number for me." He handed me a piece of paper with a phone number written on it. I read the number aloud as he dialed, then heard him begin talking. He said, "Called you to see if you'd let me come by and mess around. My mother is in a home. She can't walk. My brother and I are on two hundred acres with no one to talk to. His wife left him. I got no wife. That's why I'm calling. I got a new brick house and two hundred acres." The difference between us is that he'd made a realistic assessment of matters, and had a sense of possibilities and limits. As for me, I assessed little or nothing, but just wanted to record my thoughts, even the most negligible of them, like a poet.

May 27, '78

Living in New York you're constantly aware that much of what you know is popularly known, and much that you feel is what others feel. This voluminous knowing and feeling means you're made of popularities, or immensities of used feeling, which is like used clothing, and you're also subject to immensities of secondary experience as you go amid the crowds in streets and subways and theaters and museums and parks knowing what's known, feeling what's felt, and you're confident that you're a regular person, and this makes you both humble and massively righteous.

Since a language obliges you to echo the past every time you use it, you see why some say language uses you. When learning a new language you must submit, like the most abject slave, to its rules and capricious irregularities. The power of language can make people crazy.

May 28, '78

Spent the day with The Couple. She leans against him and touches him constantly, interrupts him midsentence, and even talks alongside him as he talks, making it impossible to understand what he is saying. He starts to tell a story. She tells it. He starts to tell me the plot of a movie, and she fills in details he omits. He has an idea, she sees what he intends and rushes to the conclusion. During her interruptions he grins, lets her shine. He doesn't resist her touching. He is pleased by its familial warmth, its puppylike intimacy, and he likes his own passive wallowing beneath her aggressive adoration and assimilation of his being. Their public sensuality and inter-twining makes an impression of perpetual lubriciousness and avail-ability, and it seems as though anybody could have either of them.

June 7, '78

Lunch with Frank at the Faculty Club. He talked about the simi-larity of olfactory and visual systems, and how sensation is chan-neled and selectively denied by higher centers of the brain. To perceive anything is to deny other things. This suggests the phys-iological basis of irony. All rhetorical forms probably have a physi-ological basis. Maybe every sentence, every word begins in your muscles and nerves, the molecular stuff, exactly the stuff that makes a continuum of you and the surrounding insensate material world. Stones, water, sunlight, air, skin—become—sensation, thought, po-etry, music, etc. Reality flows from things through sensation into words. "You" means nothing but history, place, weather. No lan-guage can be translated into another.

June 22, '78

Big dream last night. A man wearing a dark suit sits at a table with me, talking, watching me. Gradually and obliquely he conveys a message that explains my present situation. The message is that I'm dead. As usual I don't focus on the fact, but begin to wander behind it, looking for the real message, and I begin to suppose not that I'm dead but that this is a delicate piece of information and the man wants me to receive it calmly. Not for one moment do I stop with the fact of my death and focus on it. Meanwhile the surrounding life is sensual. Women walk by in shorts and skimpy bathing suits. We're in a tropical café.

You don't know who is looking at you, but it's certain that you're being looked at, closely observed, analyzed, and judged by a mind

better than yours, far more worthy of attention, not to mention respect and love, a fearsome mind.

June 26, '78
Berkeley Writers' Conference. Isaac and Alma Singer came to dinner. He said that, in translating his Yiddish to English, he does much
of the job because the translators don't know Yiddish. He said some
things are lost and some things are gained. I listened to every word,
expecting a revelation. Singer was having a good time just talking.
Alma seemed to have heard much of what he said before, and was
less easily amused than the rest of us.

Singer said he never gives quotes for book jackets, and then he
talked about a friend who writes biographies which are always
about people whose lives don't inspire readers; for example, one biography is about a man who raised dogs in New Jersey. Singer
looked at everyone sadly. Could he give a quote for this book
jacket?

During a blizzard in Warsaw, Singer was approached by a man who
asked the way to a certain street. Singer pointed left. The man hurried away to the left and vanished in the blizzard. An instant later
Singer said he realized the street was to the right, not the left. Singer
shrugged and said, "It's the only thing in my life for which I feel
guilty. I still feel guilty." I said, "Don't feel guilty. It was me. I forgive you."

Singer said, "There is only one Kafka and one Joyce in a century.
A dozen Kafkas would be a catastrophe." A dozen Joyces would
make no difference to Singer, but Kafka is a territorial competitor.

June 29, '78

I gave the longest reading I'd ever given, nearly an hour. Singer was in the audience. There was lots of laughter. Afterward he said, "You're funny and I'm funny. We should go on the road."

Singer and Alma had an argument at dinner over the color of the car that drove them from Buenos Aires to the resort, and also argued over the make of the car. She said it was a red Ford. He insisted it was a black Lincoln. They had been the guests of Argentina's auto king. Singer said, "There is no such thing as a red Ford." With this assertion he ended the argument. Earlier he said there were no blue jays. Alma ignored him. She said, "The birds in California look so fat, and they sound so satisfied."

Singer told a story about accidentally dropping a bottle of ink on a new chartreuse rug, and Alma finding him on his hands and knees cleaning the rug. He said, "If I ever want to make her crazy I need only a bottle of ink." He then said, "There is no insurance you can buy against old age." From the ink bottle to old age, from comedy to pathos.

July 1, '78

Julian says at some moment while courting it becomes wonderful and he wishes it could last forever and he didn't have to go through with all the rest. It's no trouble physically, he says, only spiritually. He cannot bear the emotional consequences of sex. Has seen all that too many times.

July 2, '78

Played tennis at Herb Sandler's. Afterward I asked if he could tell me anything about a certain businessman who lives in Aberdeen, Washington. I said he's an old friend from Ann Arbor. He was very unconventional, not interested in the business world, an outlaw. Now claims he is a lawyer, and made a fortune in real estate. We haven't seen each other in years. He was a close friend, but I don't believe his success story. Wants me to visit, see for myself.

July 3, '78
Herb phoned. As far as a bank is concerned, Burt Welcher is a good loan risk and everything he says about himself is true.

Aug. 19, '78
One who repeats what you say virtually as you say it.
One who interrupts.
One who uses a hundred words where ten would do.
One who laughs during his own remarks and nods at you
    constantly seeking agreement and confirmation and approval.
One who shuts up suddenly, goes blank, broods.
One who probes your least remark, looking for personal depths,
    revelations, etc.
One who understands you and sympathizes much in excess of
    what is natural.
One who compulsively makes cynical downbeat remarks.
One who is oppressively earnest.
One who exaggerates everything so much that he seems to lie.
One who flatters and praises and makes you bored and
    embarrassed and angry.
One who touches you.
One who asks you to repeat yourself though you've been clearly
    heard and understood.
One who asks you to repeat the joke you told him a month ago
    so that the others now might hear it, though the situation
    and the mood are very different.
One who denies what you say, and refuses to believe you.

One who is your sudden friend—if your name is William he calls
you Bill.

One who laughs mechanically, and makes you feel more amusing
than you are, though his eyes are flat and far away.

One who seems to sneer at your remarks, openly to sneer.

One who says little but responds precisely to what you say.

One who plays with your words, turning them into gibberish.

One who asks a question, then leaves the room as you answer.

One who raises his voice as you speak, overriding your remarks.

One who becomes furious when people fail to agree with him.
He thinks they fail to appreciate his seriousness and
repeatedly says, "I mean it," as if that were a fact critical to his
argument.

One who feels contempt for an idea because he understands it.
To make an idea difficult is the only defense against such
types.

One who, while listening to Bartók, thinks of himself as listening
to Bartók. All day long this putz finds reasons to approve of
himself.

Sept. 4, '78

I lose my temper. Ethan says nothing, withdraws to his room. Eventually, I follow and sit beside him on his bed, and try to explain myself and apologize. Finally, I give him a ten-dollar bill. He looks
pleased but says, "Now I feel guilty." A few moments later he has a
stomachache.

Sept. 16, '78

Flew to Seattle. Burt met me at the airport. I didn't recognize him
until he stepped in front of me and held out his hand and said my
name. He was wearing round eyeglasses and a wig, which made him
look much younger. As we drove to Aberdeen and he kept on talk-

ing, his familiar voice and personality came back, and I began to feel comfortable despite his silly wig. But it wasn't until we got to his house that old Burt returned fully to my memory. We'd just come through the door when the phone rang. Burt spoke to someone for a few minutes. He then told me the call was from one of his tenants, a woman who demanded that he have her front doorstep fixed. She said that she wouldn't pay rent if he didn't. Burt told her it would be done tomorrow. He told me that when the step is fixed, he will ask her permission to have more work done. He said she will think she intimidated him by threatening not to pay rent, and that he now wants to do more work on the house to please her. She will give him permission. Burt said he will be humble and effusively grateful for her permission. She will gloat over the extra work he is doing. Burt said he will have workmen in her house morning and night, beginning tomorrow, and they will tear the place apart. He said she will have no peace, and the work will last for months. But she will believe it's worth it. When the work is finished, Burt said, he will sell the house immediately and evict her. I heard old Burt in the tone of his voice, the sympathy he felt for the woman. He suffered with her as he turned the knife, and turned the knife.

Michael doesn't take to Burt and Burt feels similarly about Michael. They don't talk to me about each other. Two friends of mine don't like each other. The psychological axiom is: Things drawn to the same thing are repelled by each other.

Photos of semi-naked women in magazines, movies, and advertisements suggest men need erotic stimulation because they aren't much interested in sex, and women aren't much interested in anything else. But the truth is that really modern people are far more interested in the packaging than what's inside.

Sept. 26, '78

I told Bluma there is a kid in one of my classes who sits in the first row and picks his nose during my lecture. It's driving me mad. I don't know what to do about it. I can't say anything to him in class or after class. Bluma recommends that I make an announcement: "Many of you out there are picking your nose."

Sept. 29, '78

The boys go back to their mother and I get low. If I try to say what's bothering me, I feel that I'm violating the integrity of the feeling, or worse, using it to have an effect on somebody. The very particular thing that accounts for my depression was hearing Ethan greet Priscilla with "Hi, Mom." That's all. "Hi, Mom" broke my heart.

I was invited to a literary conference in Hawaii, which was held in Volcano, a town on the Big Island at the rim of the volcano's enormous crater.

Jan. 18, '79

Two interesting writers, Kathy Gable, who teaches in a classy private school, and Louise, who does a little farming. Louise says she took some photos in the street in Hilo and then was followed by a "local moke." When she saw the prints, she recognized the moke. He was in the background of one print leaning over a car window. Some other guys were in the car. Louise could tell they were in the midst of a transaction. The local moke was looking straight at the camera. Then she became frightened. She knew it was about heroin. She had to get to the guy, convince him that the picture was an accident and she was no threat. But if she brought herself to his attention, it might be worse than if she did nothing. Women are good storytellers. Louise is exceptionally good. She talks simply, an even tone, doesn't dramatize, and has a thousand stories about her daily life, and flows easily from one to another. She told me the plot of a novel about an Egyptian princess and said she was carried around in her "esophagus." I said, "sarcophagus," but I liked the way she said "esophagus." It was part of her music, the way she talked.

Feb. 2, '79

Berkeley. I asked David Reid to come to dinner. He was going to buy spareribs and go home alone. While I was preparing a salad, and Brenda was slicing an eggplant, the phone rang. It was David Levine, Brenda's old boyfriend. He asked if I'd like to go to a Warriors game against the Celtics. I wanted to go, but David Reid was coming to dinner. Besides, I told myself I was tired, and had work to do. A ball game would be a waste of time. Levine said, "You'll see Cowens and McAdoo, tremendous offensive power." I decided to go. I would also see Jojo White play against his former team for the first time. I left the house and drove as far as Euclid Avenue, and then turned back. In the house again, I said, "I won't enjoy the game." Brenda said, "You will enjoy it. Go." She assured me that David Reid wouldn't mind. "Now you're letting David Levine down." The question became which David would be let down worse? It was easiest for me to deny my own pleasure; that is, my imagined pleasure in the game. But now I didn't know if I really wanted to go. I couldn't even remember if I enjoyed watching basketball games, though I'd watched them constantly since I was fifteen years old and played high-school varsity. But I didn't want to look forward to the tremendous pleasure of being there, because it seemed insensitive and self-indulgent if I would stand up David Reid. But David Reid was late. He deserved no consideration. I decided then I should go to the game, but still felt bad about going. I went to the game. Driving home, I thought of stopping at David

Reid's place, and did. I apologized for having gone to the game, which I had enjoyed very much. Maybe I wanted to apologize for having enjoyed the game. I loved seeing into the action, the patterns of the plays, and the beautiful flow of a player's style. It turned out that David wasn't upset. He said, "You couldn't have done that to a relative or a new friend." He made it all seem funny. The memory of the game stays with me, my pleasure in seeing how good Cowens was. I hadn't appreciated him enough on TV. His excellent choice of shots. Always in the right place, giving stability to the team.

Feb. 28, '79

Peter says there is a lot at stake for a married person making a pass at someone. His or her identity—*Married*—is poignantly felt as such in sexual matters. He started thinking out loud: "If the lives of the couple did not overlap, and there were no communication—short of divorce—but only money can make this possible. So forget it." He made a good point about *Married*.

March 3, '79

The Couple. He sometimes interrupts her as she talks, and then refines her point in much detail, as if she hadn't made it nearly clear enough or else had gone wrong in an important way evident to him, if not to anyone else. She waits until he is finished, and then, as if he'd said nothing, continues precisely where she'd been stopped. "As I was saying about . . ." She never seems the least confused or irritated, and never criticizes him. She accepts him just as he is, letting him interrupt her and criticize her, which he does frequently. When he makes jokes at her expense, she smiles pleasantly, as if she were really enjoying his idea of her. Nothing he does visibly upsets her, or makes her change herself, not even when he is stoned and vicious, or when he philanders publicly. She has invincible dignity, and goes on with her life from one day to the next. She never takes drugs, or indulges in any other form of fashionable self-pity, or even thinks of herself as a survivor. Some people actually blame his suicidal debauchery on her steadiness, though it would make more sense to call her steadiness a reaction to him.

May 1, '79
Berkeley. I forgot that her husband was in the room, and that I was unlikely to see her again, and that she was twenty years older than me. She said little, but had a genius for listening, and I saw pleasure in her eyes, making me feel delicious to myself. In a voice faintly ravished, she said, "Where do you people get your energy?" She meant Jew. Big deal. Given her ethereal fragility and high-class facial bones, I also had an idea of her. I went home elated, as if I were in love. In other circumstances, we might have ravished our ideas of each other.

June 9, '79
The British colleague drew me into his office, eager to tell me something. We talked for a few minutes, and then he said it: "People will hate you." He was smiling with nasty cheer. Apparently, he'd been pondering my nature and arrived at this conclusion. He smiled with a strange intimacy, encouraging me to agree with him, accept a truth, relish the pain.

"Why?"

"Because you're spontaneous."

He means I have no manners. It's probably true, but I'd never say anything so painful to him or anyone. He had manners and yet I had the eerie impression that he thought he was being, for the moment, like what he imagined I am—without manners. He felt simpatico. I could almost taste it, the relation of intimacy and sadism.

Sept. 1, '79

I see a bird way up high. How tiny, earthbound, and remote I am.

The moment I take a strong clear position I begin to suspect that I'm wrong, which has nothing to do with truth, but is a form of social cowardice. I own a house and car, etc. Property makes you cautious. When I had nothing, I got into fistfights.

To take care of myself for the sake of myself is to be more separate from myself than if I take care of others.

I went for a walk before dawn. Black sky, no colors, and most of Berkeley didn't yet exist. Then a man appeared in the streetlights, hurtling toward me along the sidewalk. He looked to be in his fifties. He wore a gray sweatshirt, shorts, and sneakers. His knees were heavily taped, his face white and haggard. He was a runner, probably in good health, but he looked near death. Hundreds must be running in the darkness, in a trance of pain.

In the South Pacific—Fiji, Tahiti, Hawaii—great warriors never showed up for a meal without bringing a body. We bring a bottle of wine today, a torso.

Sept. 10, '79

I had to return Jake's house key, so I phoned him at the office. He said, "Just bring it to the house. My wife should be there. In the event that she's dead, stick it in her mouth." He was funny and sharp, which made me forget he is drinking himself to death.

I drove my sons from California to Pittsburgh and left them at their mother's house. It was Christmas Eve. I went on to New York by myself.

Christmas Day, Dec. 25, '79

I'm alone in Johnstown, Pa., lucky to be alive after trying to drive the turnpike to New York. I drove very slowly, worried about skidding. Whenever a truck passed and splattered the car, my windshield became a sheet of gray ice. I had to stop each time and scrape the window clean while parked on the shoulder of the road in the dark, in freezing wind. I was scared and very miserable about my life and feeling plain unlucky until I saw the exit, and left the highway and found the Holiday Inn. They had a vacant room. There is a God. Things will be O.K. Amazing how a warm clean room can change your idea of yourself and your view of the world.

Blond woman and black man, in their mid-thirties, having breakfast at the table next to mine in the Holiday Inn. She talks, talks. He nods, mutters occasionally. I hear her say, "That was different, completely different." I gather that she's talking about eras of football. She is very intense, as if trying to prove she is more knowledgeable than he is about football. He seems to have no opinions. She talks about famous runners. I hear her say, "Did you ever see his thighs? He couldn't be stopped with those thighs. And he's a great person, too. A good human being. He has sincerity, dedication, and that's it in a nutshell." The man nods, letting her know he heard what she said. He doesn't agree or disagree. He spent the night with her, and hadn't figured on this breakfast. Why is she raving about football at eight o'clock on Christmas morning? There is an imploring note in her voice. That's what he hears, I think, not all her ideas about

football, or the stuff about somebody who is a good human being
full of sincerity and dedication. He doesn't give a damn about football. He understands that she desperately wants him to be sincere
and dedicated. He's thinking nobody ever just gets laid.

At another table two boys smoke. Their thin pale hands are twitchy.
One of the boys complains about the table. He wants another table,
near the window. The other one suffers prettily. Their knees touch.

Jan. 14, '80
I'd parked a few blocks from my mother's apartment building. She
insisted that I bring my car closer and park it in front of her building. It would be safer there. So I moved the car. In the morning, I
went out to move my car again but didn't see it. I supposed I'd
parked it elsewhere and forgotten. I walked up and down the block,
but didn't see my car. A long time passed before I let myself believe
that my car had been stolen. It takes all my willpower not to start
blaming my mother and making her feel worse than she already
does.

My mother said Marty Smith's car was stolen a few months ago.
The police could do nothing to retrieve it. He drove around the
neighborhood for two weeks looking for it and finally found it
parked in front of the police station.

Grace Paley said there is a strip shop on East 11th Street where "fine
Puerto Rican mechanics" work openly on stolen cars, showing
great initiative and a will to succeed. "A boon to the economy," she
says. She's right. More cars will be sold by the manufacturers, and
the price of parts will be kept down. Her reflections on the economy are wise. A stolen car gives work to the police, who must hire
people to keep statistical records. Thus, jobs are created by stolen

cars, and they stimulate business for computer manufacturers. Everything related to stolen cars nourishes our economic system, from the small-time thief to the fine mechanics in the strip shop to the police and statisticians and insurance companies and the manufacturers of cars and computers. Our system at home and abroad has always required criminality to maximize profit, but I want my car back and would happily see the thieves flayed and impaled.

Jan. 15, '80
Dinner with Gwenn. She talked about her lover's self-indulgence and indifference to time. "Says he'll call. Doesn't." She wants him to make a commitment. He doesn't know what he wants. "He's had no real experience," she says. "Born rich. Never suffered." They began as friends, then became sexually passionate. He began to draw away. She wants a commitment because she has very little time if they're going to have children. He thinks only about his feelings, how far he is able to indulge them. What saves her from depression are brains and good looks, but also her job, which leaves her no time for her feelings, but she doesn't neglect them. She gives an hour a week to her feelings when she sees her psychotherapist. Gwenn says, "I need some terrific man for about forty-eight hours." Her psychotherapist advises her not to close off the possibilities, and to take the affair in stride. "Add it to your life," he says. Gwenn is in love. If she takes it in stride, is it love? What kind of an affair includes no risk of pain? Her psychotherapist must want to lay her, but I'd never say that to her.

I went to Birmingham, Alabama, with Brenda and Louisa, my wife and baby daughter, to teach at the University of Alabama, for one semester.

Feb. 26, '80 (Birmingham)

Every time I seem the least dissatisfied, somebody says, "It's too bad you'll be gone before spring. It's really beautiful in the spring. It all comes up." Complaining means you need attention, but I only complain about things that are beyond help, and for which no amount of attention would do me any good.

I missed the lunch at Christian's. The baby-sitter, a local black girl, had to take her own baby to the hospital, and she couldn't get here on time. I sit here in irritation and disappointment looking at my baby. From her little mouth, cottage cheese dribbles. I see myself as the man in the suit who can't get to a lunch with Birmingham muckymucks, and then think none of my friends in Berkeley would have missed that lunch. They don't miss anything. But I prefer the baby. I don't understand my irritation and disappointment, or how a person can get to be—in his feelings as well as behavior—something he isn't and never was and doesn't want to be.

Mar. 4, '80

I didn't get to lunch and then last night didn't get to the dinner party. Started out driving with fever in black rain and didn't see the Mountainbrook exit. I returned to campus and went to my office in confusion and despair and phoned and begged off without confessing my failure to see the exit. Hours later, I still feel guilty because I didn't really want to go to the dinner party.

Mar. 5, '80

Their guilt sets in the moment they make a commitment. "Can you be there at eight?" I say, and they say yes but their eyes accumulate shadow and they seem to be trying to think what all they must do before eight. I know they have already begun to suppose it won't matter if they arrive at eight-fifteen or eight-thirty. I worry about seeming too northern-east-coast-New-York and, I daresay, Jewish, ever since I heard someone on the radio describe a person as "east coast in manners. Direct." He meant pushy, New York, etc. . . . The agreed-upon time for meeting, eight P.M. or whatever, means always more or less around that time. It makes sense. Any commitment might lead to failure, disgrace, anger, misunderstanding, and very difficult tests of affection. Why should they live according to a schedule, or feel oppressed by casual ill-considered commitments? Just being conscious all day is a troublesome condition. The important thing is that folks look clean and neat, and are always ready to promise to be somewhere, or to do this or that, and always be polite. Larry Wharton told me about seeing an old man with a cane standing in a parking lot, and some car pulled up behind him and honked for him to get out of the way. He turned around and smashed the windshield with his cane. The car drove on by, not wanting more trouble. The old man might have been carrying a gun, the guarantor of politeness.

Larry says he's had "students who can tell you the name of every football player in Alabama's defensive backfield, first and second string, but they never heard of Hitler."

Having dinner in the Chinese restaurant, I asked for chopsticks, and the waiter brought them. I was using them when I noticed a couple at a nearby table staring at me with pure hatred. I put down the chopsticks and picked up my fork and continued eating like an

American. The couple stopped staring. Southern hicks, maybe, but I've seen much the same thing in New York, in sophisticated circles, and far more vicious.

Mar. 7, '80

During the interview with the gorgeous blond reporter from the town paper, I asked her too many questions. She didn't discourage conversation, and told me about herself and her family, and how her mother had been in love with a man for twenty years before she left her husband, the reporter's father. She said that she goes to visit her father, and cooks dinner for him. "Would you like some spaghetti, Daddy?" she said, imitating herself. She sounded sweet and unbearably sad. I imagined the poor man eating spaghetti, mystified by what had happened to him. I knew that I'd lose sleep thinking about the blonde. Sit in your office in blue jeans, instead of a jacket and tie, and you can ruin your life. I said, "I think I'm falling in love." She said, "Me, too."

Mar. 12, '80

Rainy, cold, gloomy day. I leave tomorrow and I'm all packed, but there is always something more to do. It will present itself the minute I start out the door. I'm sorry about leaving Birmingham, saying goodbye to all the people, especially the Perlises, Whartons, the Honorable Josh Mullinses, and Bernie Feld, Laura Milner, the students in my night class, and Mary Brown of Browns, Alabama, one of the best writers I know. She raises soybeans, goes to church, writes stories, and, in her nice house way out in the country, all alone, this eighty-year-old white lady listens to Charlie Parker and John Coltrane records on her phonograph.

Tami talked about her romance with an older man and her father's threat to shoot him, though the man is a boss in the Alabama mafia and more likely to shoot her father. She had a glossy Vaselined area around her mouth, and a low-keyed southern manner. She said I was a good lecturer. "You could be a preacher," she said, "and you wouldn't even have to believe any of it." She lives outside of Birmingham in a small community of houses scattered about farmland. The place had a name and a church but I didn't see an actual place. She thought about showing me a small town nearby, but was too frightened. She said, "Police cars have been known to enter that town and never come out." The residents descend from Tennessee families displaced by the TVA when they built the dam. They never forgave the United States government, and have no respect for authority. If you're driving a car with northern plates you're liable to get shot. So we didn't go to that town, but drove back to Birmingham, exchanged addresses, and said goodbye without kissing.

 *I drove home to Berkeley from Birmingham, making stops along the way at Iowa City, Colorado Springs, and Lincoln, Nebraska. I gave readings to cover my expenses. Brenda and Louisa flew home without me.*

May 15, '80
Berkeley. Met Peter for lunch. He had good news. His former wife remarried. His happiness was apparent; his relief. Another man might feel hurt, jealous, angry, etc. It's possible also to feel nothing. It's possible to feel almost anything, but if you believe feelings are

less important than right, wrong, good, bad, proper, improper, lawful, or licentious behavior, people think you're inhuman, sick, deficient in basic sentiments, etc.

I like Phoebe's face—thick black wavy hair, white skin, freckles, dark blue eyes, small fine features with a serious rather than cute expression. She's pretty but the seriousness of her expression makes her unconventionally pretty, almost as if being pretty is tedious, a burden, since she is a thoughtful person. She talks about Hank in a lazy, sophisticated, L.A. nasal voice, and slouches in her chair. Sounds bored, or world-weary, as if Hank weren't all that important, just another burden. In fact, she's wildly obsessed. Her tone is a lie. She thinks of nothing but Hank. I cut her short, saying, "He's too old for you." Her eyes go vague. Now she is too pretty to understand my brutal remark. She retreats into pretty-being, so pretty she can be stupid whenever she likes. I become impatient. I say, "You'll understand when you move in with Hank and he walks around the house in his underwear, belching and farting." Her eyes click as if she took a picture. She says nothing.

Am I jealous? Does it matter to me if she sleeps with Hank? If so, it's theoretical jealousy. There is nothing at stake. She happens to be pretty. I like to look at her, which doesn't get in the way, as far as I'm concerned, of her interesting mind and L.A. manner, which is ridiculous but witty, nonetheless, and I get a kick out of it. She talks to me about Hank, always in that slow, nasal voice. I listen. I don't encourage it. She sounds not only weary, but almost sick, as if she has a disease she can't do anything about. Phoebe of moods. Since we're not having an affair, maybe there is nothing else for us to talk about aside from the affair she is having. Maybe there is nothing else to talk about ever, if compared to having an affair.

May 20, '80

Lunch with Hank at the faculty club. Phoebe told him that I said he walks around in his underwear, belching and farting. He was laughing. I'll never talk to Phoebe again.

May 30, '80

Memory: When I finished a draft of my dissertation, I asked Elliott Gilbert to read it. He read it overnight and came striding into my office in the morning.

"Congratulations," he boomed.

"What do you think?"

"What you wrote sounds exactly like a dissertation."

Ten years later, I still feel gratitude and affection.

May 31, '80

The Couple: He thinks he is blamed for not being able to do what he wants to do, which is, more than anything else, to make her happy. He imagines himself talking to her, trying to understand her distress, but he can't hear himself. Neither of them hears the other. You could be happy, he thinks, if he could understand what to do, but he then thinks: No. Happy is taboo. There's no use trying to give her what she needs if what she needs is to feel it isn't being given. This is the truth. Thinking ends here. Time to go away.

Characters: A lawyer suffers grief because he lost a tennis game at his club. He lies on the couch, refusing to talk to his wife, refusing dinner, refusing sleep. He has a family and earns a million-plus a year, but loses at tennis and he has nothing, is living a lie, and might as well be dead. Tell him otherwise, he says, "You're not me." Not every man is a compulsive winner. Minsky, my accountant, tells me in statistical terms why it is impossible to beat the odds at black-jack, then goes to Tahoe and tries to beat the odds at blackjack. He's had to take a second mortgage on his house. A scrawny bad-tempered little guy, he gambles against impossible odds. Hilary went with him to Tahoe and watched. She doesn't bitch, just lights an-other cigarette. I imagined them driving back to San Francisco, Minsky at the wheel and Hilary beside him, looking out the side window, wondering if she should get a job. The dark philosopher Heracleitus said the road up is the road down. He is talking about existential discontent. Up, down—it's the same thing.

The Couple: She said of the baby-sitter, "She sure is beautiful." When he drove the baby-sitter home, he found himself turned on. By what? His wife's idea of the girl as beautiful? His wife was more attractive, but he was trembling with excitement and then felt like a criminal driving home, and was anxious to be there, free of this insanity. The next day the baby-sitter phoned him at work and said, "How's your wife?" The contempt in her voice was hard. He didn't know who it was, then realized. The excitement came surging back along with the memory of last night. He said, "Between you and me, there was almost a big mistake." She said, "I'll tell my grand-children about it." The girl was about half his age, but she seemed emotionally more mature than himself.

June 10, '80

Phoebe comes to my office. Ever since Hank told me she'd re-peated what I said, I've been angry at her. I say, "What's new?" and won't reveal my anger until she starts talking about Hank. She doesn't start. She tells me she was caught shoplifting in a women's clothing store on Telegraph Avenue. A policeman led her from the store in handcuffs, into the noontime crowd, the most degrading experience of her life. "You poor thing," I said, thinking she'd been punished for the business about Hank. I didn't like her face anymore.

I've written little because there is so much not to be said. I like Charles Wright's line: "There is so little to say and so much time to say it in."

I like Donald Justice's sentence: "All the devices of sound tend toward meaninglessness." I say something funny to the little kid, and make her laugh, and she touches my mouth. She wants to feel where it came from, the reason for her laughing. Among devices of sound is the mouth.

Simone Weil thinks fiction is immoral except for Homer, Shakespeare, Tolstoy, and a few others. That she starved herself to death doesn't mean she's wrong, only consistent.

The poet who read yesterday at Berkeley said, "I don't like great poetry. It's too finished. It makes me feel it doesn't need me." Ridiculous, I thought, but then thought, No; the idea that great poetry doesn't need her is very good. It doesn't need anybody, and whether or not you like it is irrelevant.

I was invited to teach a writing class at Johns Hopkins University. When I arrived in Baltimore I had to go dashing around an unfamiliar city looking for a house to rent before the term begins. I stayed with Stanley and Adrienne Fish. I told Stanley that nobody

at the university was helping me find a place to live. Stanley said he'd
once been invited to MIT to give a talk and nobody met him at the air-
port or took him to dinner or put him up for the night.

Feb. 1, '81

Feldheim says he wants to rent his house. He has two TV sets and
leaves them on all day, even with nobody in the house, and he
boasts that he never watches TV. In fact he doesn't. He's too worried and jumpy. He wears his overcoat in the house, and walks from
room to room with his hands in the pockets, shoulders slumped.
Within minutes of our meeting, I knew he was seriously depressed.
In him it registers as feeling cold and keeps him moving about. His
business is failing, he says, but he thinks mainly about his wife, not
his business. She helps make him agitated. After Feldheim showed
me his house and I said I would rent it, we went back to his car. He
said, "I don't believe my wife is a trollop," as if he assumed that I did.
I'd met her only minutes previously while touring the rooms. She
went about with her blouse open, as if it were a style, exposing
sweet little breasts. Feldheim, wearing his overcoat, seemed vicari-
ously to cover her nakedness. She stood too close when we were introduced. Her eyes are violet. Every gesture was flirtatious, or
somehow eroticized. Her posture, her voice, and the way she moved
carried intimations of something not immediately relevant. Beyond her breasts and intimations, she hasn't much conversation. I
suppose Feldheim married her, despite her brainless manner, because she is sexy-looking. With his eyes open, he married her, and
now they're married. If he were blind, he'd never have done it.
Both of them are aware of his mistake. She is exacerbating it to
punish him, maybe. She doesn't have his smarts, but she knows
how to feed his self-destructive passion. Maybe he requires it of her.
He gave her a comfortable life in a fancy Baltimore neighborhood.

Another man might have burned down the house and hanged himself long ago. Their baby looks like their marriage.

Feldheim didn't say much, but, as if he assumed I understood everything, he quickly became personal, talking about his wife, his failing business, his reasons for having to leave Baltimore and rent the house. He had a strange dignity. I liked him, and I was sorry about his troubles. I also felt anxious about the rental agreement. Being subject to powerful impulses, Feldheim might suddenly change his mind and cancel the agreement if only to feel like a man of decisive character. I remembered the guy upstate married to the Puerto Rican beauty queen. She didn't want him along when she and her girlfriends left the party and went dancing. Drunk, he stumbled after them out of the house. The girls hit him and pushed him away. He kept pressing among them as they walked to the car until he slipped and fell in the mud. They left him there and drove off. He came back into the house, mud up and down the side of his overcoat and pants. Without removing the overcoat, he resumed drinking and conversing with the guests, unashamed of his condition. What else could he do? He lived miles away and his wife had the car. I remembered him because of the overcoat. Like Feldheim, he had a pretty wife and wore an overcoat in the house.

Feb. 2, '81
In Kafka's diaries, he writes: "The woman who, only because she walks on the arm of her fiancé, looks quietly around." You can talk about the meaning of the line forever. Aside from that, it's true.

Hamlet talks about Gertrude's shoes. She wore them to her husband's funeral and so little time has passed that they're still in good shape but she's married again. Socrates talks about his new shoes, saying he bought them to go to a banquet at the home of a handsome man. Van Gogh's painting of shoes is also about social inauthenticity, but there is nothing ironical in it or the idea of labor.

The television or radio plays incessantly. Voices and images usurp people's interior lives. Media-besotted, they don't know the difference between within and without, self and not-self. They live inside out, or outside in. They're saved from entertainment only by terror. This kind of thing was noticed in the Old Testament, which was long before television.

Driving from Johns Hopkins in Baltimore to my mother's place in New York, I missed a turn to the Delaware Memorial Bridge and got lost. I felt incompetent and very upset, but stopped at a McDonald's for a psychological hamburger, and soon calmed down and was on my way.

The day was complicated with chores—buying insurance, fixing broken household machines, appointments around town. I did nothing for its own sake, and wanted only to get things over with. Even meetings with friends. I wanted to get them over with, just as with chores, and I thought I live from moment to moment with no gratification except in endings. Saying a goodbye has become a pleasure.

Feb. 3, '81
Samantha's boyfriend went to Europe and she came to visit us in Baltimore. She told us that her boyfriend brought her coffee and neglected to put milk in it. "We're through," she cried. "After three years you still don't know that I take milk in my coffee. Fuck you." She was shouting, reliving his failure, her loud denunciation.

The woman at our dinner party had an Austrian accent and a sweet, sensuously sentimental tone, reminiscent of Viennese pastry, which remained unchanged all evening no matter what she said, rising when she talked of happy things and rising just the same when she talked about the man who read "so many books" and looked "so dear carrying them about" and had liver cancer. Samantha then gave a high-spirited laughing account of brutally bad treatment she had received from her boyfriend. If you didn't know English, you'd suppose she was talking about something that made her deliriously happy.

I don't literally complain, but Brenda says, "I can't listen to this anymore." I asked for no sympathy, only conversation. My description was maybe a touch nerve-racking. One could suppose I was complaining, but there is a difference. I need a new style, a sort of bland conversational manner.

Feb. 4, '81
Brenda and Samantha were in the kitchen making cookies. "My boyfriend's friend made a pass at me," said Samantha. She then talked about her principled restraint, and said her boyfriend would break up with her if anything happened between his friend and her. He'd keep his friend, not her. She didn't want to lose her boyfriend, and said she'd get his friend later if she wanted him. Her boyfriend is still in Europe. She lives in the same building in Manhattan as his friend. Every night she climbs down the fire escape from her bedroom to his and slides naked into bed with him. Then they don't literally do it. The closer they come to doing it, and then don't do it, and the more often they don't do it, the more it isn't done and the more she hasn't betrayed her boyfriend. Few people have ever not done a certain thing as often or as much as they haven't. As Samantha talked she dipped her pinky in the cookie dough, quickly licked her finger clean, and kept on talking, her gesture so quick it seemed she hadn't done it. Same with the boyfriend's friend—not

doing it. Not doing it again and again. She said her boyfriend was never jealous when she had a crush on a guy, but became enraged if she slept with him. He said, "You can't control your feelings. You can control your behavior." She says it's feelings that matter. Anyone can sleep with anyone, but you have feelings only for certain people.

Feb. 5, '81

In artworks things appear as-seen-by-the-artist. In the world things simply exist. In child art, they also appear simply to exist.

Possible story: Sonya says she didn't know her husband had been unfaithful. She is dismayed, deeply hurt. Others can't understand how she managed not to know, or can say that she didn't know. Her husband made no secret of it. Everyone knew. Except her. It's hard to believe. The other woman, when confronted, tells Sonya that her husband's infidelity is Sonya's problem. Sonya repeatedly says she didn't know. Everyone assumed she knew. There was nothing anyone felt obliged to tell her, and nothing anyone could discuss. It's such a cliché—"the last to know." Knowing and not knowing are more important in regard to sexual fidelity than anything else, even personal health. People dread going to the doctor, but don't hesitate to read a lover's mail or diary.

Sustaining a fragile structure that passes for one's life. Friends won't discredit it, strangers accept it, and you needn't worry about it, and you will get through, and eventually get old and then die without having had to acknowledge, let alone live, any truth.

Feb. 10, '81

Dream: Samantha was angry. I start thinking how to protect the baby. I decide to make the baby seem less precious to me, and announce that she has bad breath. Thus, I explained to myself that Samantha is angry at us because the baby gets more attention.

Memory: A motel in west Texas. I'm checking out early. The weather is cruel and seems to know I'm leaving the motel, coming out into it as soon as I pay my bill. My boys are still in the room, reluctant to get dressed and join me in the weather. They've been fighting, smashing each other with pillows. I'm disappointed. I'd wanted to make this long drive across the country with my boys. It turns out not to be much fun. They fight with each other constantly. The sky is murky gray and purple, and resembles the skin of an eel. It feels too close, looming, big with pressure. There is a sporadic wind, a high-strung, nervous wind, like an overbred dog aquiver with impulse and no brains. The sky is moving fast. It follows me around the parking lot, and trails me indoors. Then rain hits the ground. Doesn't fall. It hits, hits, hits.

Feb. 21, '81
Insurance forms, tax forms, license applications, notices from the university administration, receipts, invoices . . . these documents tell a person who he is, what he's done, what he's worth. After a while, it's hard to remember the undocumented self. Flannery O'Connor's character the Misfit says, "They had the papers on me," and supposes he must have done something bad.

Being talked at, I sit, I slump, and feel life dribbling away. I rise, I go, followed from the room being talked at.

Feb. 22, '81
In a loud voice, Samantha reads the name on every storefront as we drive through town. I don't know how to stop her, or how to ask why she is doing that. She must feel bored. She opinionates about

matters personal to me even while I'm talking to someone else, as if to show, by interrupting me, that she is closer to me than the person I'm talking to. She talks loud, louder than anyone in the room. She laughs extravagantly at her own jokes and at things I say that aren't always intended to be funny. She talks about anyone she knows as if he or she were a good friend. She says she doesn't eat when she eats like a horse. She says she doesn't leave lights burning when she does that all the time. She says she didn't make a certain phone call when she did, and says she is studying Arabic and loves it, when she isn't and doesn't. She says she wants to be X's "friend," but then climbs through the window into his room, wearing only her nightgown. She says the baby doesn't like her. The baby likes her very much. She means she doesn't like the baby. The baby isn't paying enough attention to her, isn't mothering her.

Samantha asked if I would write a letter of recommendation for her. I said yes and asked, "Is the letter for admission to graduate school or do you need it for a job?" She said, "You don't have to do it. You have a lot else to think about. You mustn't feel obliged." I said, "I'm happy to do it, but I should know to whom the letter is addressed." She repeated herself, saying she knows I have a lot else on my mind, and she doesn't want to burden me with this, too. I said it's no trouble, I want to do it. I wanted to say, if you don't let me do it, I'll strangle you. She hardened in refusal—No, she won't burden me with anything so minor. I will have to beg for the privilege of writing the letter. I will have to raise the subject as if it were something I thought of all by myself. I feel as if I'm involved with her. In the precise sense of this word, I am involved with her. It has nothing to do with sex. Only by a few degrees am I differently involved than her boyfriend's friend. In fact, the way Samantha deals with her boyfriend's friend, being involved is antithetical to sex. This could be true even if there were plenty of sex.

March 17, '81

An interesting woman talked about dinner with her former husband. She said he'd tried to fix her up with a friend of his. Could be a good story. The triangle is an ancient dramatic situation, basic to the Iliad and Odyssey, the Bible, and Shakespeare. In the modern version the husband deliberately creates the triangle. He needs to feel jealousy—his darkest, and most exquisite, pleasure. At a party in Cupertino, I saw Ray Carver watching me dance with Marianne. He was sodden drunk, gloomy and glowering. Who knows what he imagined. I said goodnight and drove away. I won't be in one of Ray's jealous-husband stories.

Telling a story, she starts to include irrelevant detail as if she doesn't know what her story is about; she's lost, grabbing at whatever comes to mind, unable to select; or unable to deal with the authority granted by an audience, or overwhelmed by the wonderfulness of being listened to. Most people tell stories naturally, better than professional writers if they don't think they're doing it.

Francine's novel says there is a time after forty-five when romantic adventures are over, delicious illusions are impossible to sustain, and truth becomes a need. Saint Augustine says the same—first sex, then truth. He associates delicious illusions with going to the theater, a deplorable indulgence, he believes.

Nietzsche says the worst reader takes what he needs, then confuses and blasphemes all the rest. Coleridge talks about desecration, as if such readers can imagine no reading, no judgment, not their own. They rape books. But it's how they curse God. They know Coleridge is saved, and they're going to hell.

March 19, '81

Memory: I drive across the country with the boys. To me it's a great thing, seeing the country. They read comic books, sleep, or look up when I tell them there is something to see but they never look with much interest. When I was their age, I had no such experience, so I suppose they ought to be thrilled. I'm thinking of myself, then. They can tell what I expect them to feel so they feel nothing, and then I feel like a writer who is lavish in adjectives, using up the feelings before the reader has had them. The boys want the radio playing rock music. In the morning when the light is beautiful, I don't want it soiled with that noise, but after driving most of the day, I'm too tired to care. Then I can listen to anything they want.

April 8, '81

At the dinner last night, blabbing about this and that, I was unintentionally provocative. I said property owners who rent to small businesses and then take a percentage of their profits are the same as extortionists. I didn't know that Milton G. happens to be such a property owner. He became incensed. He said: "When it comes to money, questions of right and wrong don't exist. You make a profit, you're right. Money is irrelevant to moral considerations. Money is about action. The way a person gets money is action. You took classes in philosophy, my friend. I also took classes in philosophy. I know moral considerations are infinitely debatable. There is never any final knowledge, but always another angle, another consideration. Not so with money. With money everything is clear. It's action. Either you made it or you haven't. It's necessary to oblige people to think this way, necessary to force them to make more and more money by virtue of a tax upon their labors. This induces and perpetuates action. The investor is like another level of government. He makes things go. He charges rent for the money he invests, and then he asks for a percentage of the profit beyond the rent. Some will do better than others in regard to their investments, but you want to know something—the better ones make it possible for the others to stay in business. Think about it, my friend." I didn't think about it, but I got a kick out of him, his energy, his conviction, his feisty style.

A flier tacked to a telephone pole said Sonny Stitt will play in a bar in Fells Point. With that kind of announcement, I figured there wouldn't be much of a crowd, but the bar was almost full when I arrived, and there was a line about half a block long of people waiting to get in. I had a sense of fellowship with a couple of hundred strangers. Sonny Stitt made the bar's darkness brilliant with his horn. It was the happiest night I'd spent in Baltimore. Other times I remember with pleasure were the afternoon in Washington, D.C., at the Phillips gallery where I discovered the Soutine painting of the kids passing through a field under a violent sky. There was also the night of the crab dinner at Gunnings, wearing a bib, the long table covered with a sheet of butcher paper, and I remember the antique dealer who bought a collection of erotica from the estate of a recently deceased dentist. I called Larry McMurtry's bookstore, and told him and he bought the collection from the dealer sight unseen. The figure seemed to me high, but he said it wasn't nearly what the collection is worth. The idea of a Baltimore dentist collecting erotica all his life—it had to be valuable.

My novel The Men's Club *was published around this time. It received more attention than anything I'd ever published before. I had opportunities to publicize it on television and radio, but I've never been able to sell anything*

and I didn't think I would do the novel or myself much good. I decided to drive from Baltimore to California alone not to promote the book, and for a little while I was inaccessible, but I saw some people I knew and met a few others who became friends.

May 1, '81

Sunday in Mississippi: Elmer Hillman, Tom Sims, Raymond Leake. "Some men bring spit cups to church. Others find a pew beside the window," says Elmer. Later, walking about the ranch, I smelled something horrible. "A dead possum," said Elmer. We drove to a neighbor's place and looked at beagles for sale. If a dog won't hunt, they shoot it. Statements on the car radio driving from Louisiana to Texas: (1) "God only made two things to move—black billy goats and crawfish." (2) "A woman has to be touched eight times a day." (3) "Tight as bullfrogs in a jam jar." The first one is unintelligible. The second, which was said by a preacher, is sadistic as well as absurd. The third is good concrete imagery. All in all, it seemed to me, people growing up in the south can hardly help being good writers, assuming they don't prefer to spend their time in conversation, which of course they do.

May 5, '81

Fisher Motel, about seven miles west of Port Arthur. Met Kay and Tommy. Tommy Shook, ex-ranger, parachutist, made high-altitude jumps—25,000 feet or higher. Fought in Vietnam. Talked about the Port Arthur area, the oil refineries, rice farmers, hunting lodge, wolves, snakes, alligators, Vietnamese fishermen and their trouble with local fishermen and the KKK. Said there are about 70,000 alligators in this area. They have crawled into town and eaten dogs. This is an open season on alligators. Celebrities come down here to use the hunting lodge—Bum Phillips, Bob Hope. Talked about

Vietnam and the administration of the war, ten support troops for every combat troop, officers on six-month combat duty and then gone. Talked about his training as a ranger, a mental achievement as much as physical. Survived in the jungle. Manning a gun in a helicopter he was hit in the left eye by shrapnel. It spun him around, bloody and blinded. A solid, serious, good man, with strong feelings about the country's need for a first-rate army. He means first-rate soldiers, nothing a government can buy.

Talked to Kay. She told me about a father separated from his sons, like me, and how he sees them rarely. He's happy when they arrive, and then crashes because he spends too much time thinking about their departure. Too much pain amid the happiness. She said a father is important to sons at about the age of twelve to fifteen, but his importance is in his desire to see them. Actual seeing isn't crucial.

May 6, '81
Met David and Lecia Harmon. Invited me to dinner. Beautiful old dining room table and chairs. Shotguns in bathroom. "A burglar wouldn't look in there," said David. Talked about their right-wing politics. Talked about Lecia's sister, Mary Karr, a poet, not right-wing. Lecia phoned Mary in Boston and said I was at the table having dinner with them. Mary said she'd gone east just to seduce famous writers. The family is smart, funny, likable, and more Texas than political.

Called Lynn Nesbit in N.Y. She said not to write about the Texas scene. Not natural to me. I don't have the background or the language for physical action, violence, etc. I wondered how many Jewish writers are good with violence? Isaac Babel compares well with Flannery O'Connor, Robert Stone, or Elmore Leonard, but usually Jews lack the "mind of winter." They tend to produce sensational huffing and puffing, too much Oi Yoi, or irrelevant innerness and moral sensibility. A Jew couldn't have written the murder scene in "A Good Man Is Hard to Find," or the sex-murder in *A Flag for Sunrise.* The extended murder scene in *Mr. Sammler's Planet* is brilliant, but the intention to mean something is stronger than the drama.

May 26, '81

There should be a test you have to pass before being allowed to write book reviews. For example: How many men figure in this story about seven men? If the reviewer says "six," he might be an aging impotent drunk, a failed poet, or a horse's ass.

July 1, '81

I'm unhappy because Jesse is going back to Pittsburgh. He said I should think of it as a broken leg. It will get better. We talked a little. I told him I never spent much time with my father. I'd see him early in the morning and after dinner because he left early and came home late, and I'd see him Sundays. I'd thought I was lucky to have my professor job—so much free time to spend with my kids—but the boys now live in Pittsburgh. I asked Jesse about his friends in Pittsburgh. He said some are Jewish, "others are Jewish-ish."

Jesse is running up the block. I'm proud of my wild kid. My mother pinches my elbow, whispering, "He could fall."

July 4, '81

I go to the party in the Berkeley hills. This one wrote a book. That one is rich. I find one who seems ordinary. He is standing in a corner and has dirty fingernails. He tells me his name in a frightened voice, as if saying a nasty word. I like him immediately and relax into conversation, pleased that he is unattractive and has almost nothing to say, but it turns out that he writes a column for a national magazine on the arts and is married to Austrian royalty.

July 10, '81

I pour Kahlúa into a glass of milk, add bourbon, then light a cigarette because it's the last time I'll let myself do it—drunken blur, cigarette gas, twilight on the bay ... The moment is so pleasing, private, and completely possessed by me that I feel guilty, but then think it's all right to enjoy myself because anyone can do it. I remembered waking up at dawn at the rim of the Grand Canyon, and getting out of my car to watch the canyon emerge in shadowy blue silence, and feeling the sublimity of the slowly emerging hugeness, and then I noticed others on either side of me along the rim of the canyon, as if we'd all been called from sleep to witness. Nobody was talking or taking pictures. A happy sensation then because I wasn't the only one to see this. I forgot that I felt chilled and cramped, having slept all night in my car.

Sept. 22, '81

You're a depressed and pessimistic type, but much happier than most people because you're so often wrong—your work wasn't rejected, your greetings were returned, you passed the test, didn't get sick, came home all right, the check was in the mail, the house didn't burn down, your kid recovered, your watch wasn't stolen, the dog wasn't rabid, the noise in the dark wasn't a murderer, the plane didn't crash, you got the job, the girl, the prize, and won the race and lost the rash, the cough, the tic, the worm, the stink, the fear.

Memory: I was in Iowa City, in the Mill, drinking with David Soll. He said a woman friend of his supported a painter for twelve years. Then they took a trip to Rome. The first day there he beat her up in a hotel room and left her on the floor unconscious. She never saw him again. A girl walked by and David said to her, "If you need a massage, let me know." She smiled. Girls like David. He likes girls. He flirted while I sat there thinking about the woman in the hotel room. The Mill was crowded at the bar and tables. There was every sort of distraction, but for me the woman was still on the floor. If you tell a story you incur a responsibility. David is a natural, producing stories in extraordinary abundance. The woman finally drifted from mind and vanished in the noise and cigarette smoke. Now, years later, I remember her.

Two great stories of nonconsummation—"Gawain and the Green Knight," and Chekov's "The Kiss." Also the poem "La Belle Dame . . ." Nonconsummation used to be a subject. God forbid readers today should be denied a vicarious fuck.

Sept. 23, '81
Invited to go to Disneyland with the in-laws. Three young sailors were walking ahead of us. A creature appeared around a corner. One sailor dropped into a crouch and screamed, "Holy shit, it's Jiminy Cricket." I thought it was a child molestor. The place is swarming with them.

Memory: Fred Dupee invited me to visit him in Santa Barbara, but I couldn't make myself telephone him, set a date, ask directions, and I wanted very much to visit him.

Sept. 30, '81
Possible story: Lucy, in Lincoln, Nebraska, said that one night she slept with her best friend, a boy her age. She'd known him for years. They'd never been romantically involved with each other. After the sex he got up, dressed, and started out of the room. Lucy

watched him until he reached the door, and then she yelled at him, called him a son of a bitch, demanded that he come back. He did. He took off his clothes and got back into bed with her. Thus, she saved the friendship. They never had sex again. Lucy lived in a trailer with her mother, and made money by offering herself as a subject in psychological and medical experiments.

Bonnie hates criticism. I can't even suggest that she correct her grammar or spell a word correctly. She thinks I'm asking her to correct herself. She phoned me today and said, "I met your friend Hank. He'd like to see me again." I said, "So you don't want to see him again?"

"No, no. I do." And then, as if I were even more stupid than she imagined, she says, "Should I tell him that he and I met a year ago in Maui?"

"How embarrassing."

"And that we had a sexual encounter?"

"Worse and worse."

"He did it to me from behind."

"Can I call you later?"

In the middle of a funny story, he started laughing so hard he couldn't finish it. He took off his glasses, wiped the lenses with a handkerchief until he regained himself, and then continued. He told us about an evening in San Francisco when Beard passed out in a whorehouse and had to be carried home by three whores. Some women in the crowd began clutching each other and squealing. The very whores, I supposed, Ho, Ho, Ho.

Memory: Small Baptist church, a few hours north of Biloxi. The preacher is skinny, pale, sickly-looking. He carries his head thrust forward, roosterlike, on a scrawny neck. His sermon is delivered through a tight, fierce smile, giving his face a look of cheerful and controlled fury. He says, "You folks in church are keeping far more folks out of church." He means the congregation is smug, not reaching out to their Christian brothers and sisters. After the sermon, about forty men and women stand up in the pews, and release their voices in a powerful unity of song. They'd just been told they weren't good Christians, but they sure could sing. Later, at the coffee and cookie "fellowship," I saw the preacher's daughter, three years old, as sickly-looking as her dad, but she had scary, fire-bright, transfixing eyes. A woman came up and started talking to me. She said, "I don't like the preacher's new beard. He's growing it to hide a skin problem, but I think he should shave it off. I like to see a man's face." She wore a mask of thick makeup. Her hair was shining, like a Technicolor movie, and mangled into a "do."

July 27, '82
The house is old, full of troubles, and the cost of termite work will take much of what I earned while wasting my life writing a screenplay. It's as if the termites jumped inside me to bring home a sense of corruption.

Browsing in Black Oak Books, I pick up a book and see the photo of a woman painter who lived in the nineteenth century in the West. Her face affects me so strongly that it seems I must have known her, perhaps loved her, and we had a life together. I then felt myself sinking into the incurable misery of lost love. I shut the book before it was too late. I continued to be drawn to it, but I walked about looking at other books and I wouldn't touch it again.

The speed at which we understand jokes is astonishing, quicker than the speed of light. We also understand other things at astonishing speed. But we don't understand how we understand. Given the evidence of our heads, let alone the visible universe, there must be a God.

Oct. 7, '82
Saying whatever meanness comes to mind lest it come to mind again.

Adultery has less to do with romance and sex than with the discovery of how little we mean to each other.

When Max found out his wife had been unfaithful, he said, "She has freed me of guilt, made me clean. I can regard my own infidelities in a new light, and I can do anything I'd like. How come I'm so miserable?"

Oct. 9, '82
Party at Peter's. Everyone there was a psychotherapist; an atmosphere of restraint. Slow, carefully considered speech. Jeremy's remark about quitting psychoanalysis after six years came to mind. He'd become bored talking about himself, he said.

Oct. 10, '82
I went to Washington, D.C., for a few days to join a committee reading applications for Fulbright awards. Then I went to Alabama. In Oak Mountain Park the leaves were gray, red, yellow, and every other color, and all the colors were fallen on the ground. A few maples were still green, but most were rusty pink. I was looking at the Cahaba River in the late afternoon, watching the men fish, when Laura said, "Is everything to your liking, sir." I said, "Yes, thank you." She said, "Ma'am." I said, "Yes, thank you, ma'am."

Nov. 28, '82

Since she asked, I said I know one man who isn't married and likes women. "Would I like him?" she asks. "You might," I said, then added that he goes from one woman to another, leaving them badly disappointed. He's interested only in sex. She said, "Give him my number." She didn't suppose her fate would be like that of the other women, but it's always difficult to make a truly heterosexual man seem less than desirable.

Nov. 11, '82

Alison came by and told me about a guy in Santa Cruz with whom she'd had a three-day fling, all sex and no conversation. They had nothing in common, nothing at all to talk about. They drove around and had a drink in a bar, but never found anything to talk about, so they always went back to bed as soon as possible to have sex and avoid the agony and embarrassment of trying to talk to each other.

Had lunch at Chez Panisse with Diane Johnson and we talked for over two hours. She said that she'd been stopped for drunk driving. She'd had only two glasses of wine but did seem to be driving funny, though not because she was drunk. The cops asked her to re-cite the alphabet and she found that she couldn't get past KLMNO. They gave her another chance, but she was so scared she couldn't do it the second time either. They let her go, anyhow. She thinks it was because she had a dog in the car. It was too much trouble for them to deal with a dog. She discovered later that two tires had been punctured by vandals, irreparably damaged, which explained her funny driving.

I need someone to talk to. It can't be a psychotherapist. I need a "good" person. My problem is moral, not psychological. I don't know how to live.

Nov. 12, '82

The son of a psychiatrist tells me his father has one patient he likes, a psychic who predicts disasters and then feels responsible for them. Presumably the predictions are correct. I imagine the unhappy psychic and charmed psychiatrist. What must happen is that the psychic predicts *after the fact,* then says he knew the plane would crash. He feels responsible. He is a benificent paranoic. What if he really predicted disasters before they happened? What could the psychiatrist do? If he went about warning everyone, he'd be considered nuts. Something like this happens in the Book of Jonah when he goes about Nineveh predicting its doom.

Her station wagon has a baby seat, and she wears a wedding ring. There are pictures in her wallet of her kids and her husband. Thus, when she goes to her lover she carries things that speak of her other life, including even her diaphragm. Maybe she needs these things as reminders of her conventional moral identity. In a Mary McCarthy novel a woman wonders about using one diaphragm with different partners; a question of the same orifice doesn't arise.

Nov. 18, '82

Wild ride to the airport after long—too long—conversation in class. Arrived at 1:45, the time of departure. I parked the car in the wrong place, the flight attendants' parking, and then discovered the flight had been delayed and wasn't going to leave until 2:20. There had been some breakdown in the ground-to-air communication system. I arrived late at the Ontario airport. Ralph Angel was waiting for me, a big smoker with a clean new Honda. Neatly dressed. Long slender face. After the reading at San Bernardino, off to dinner with Ralph, Denny Louie, and Rod Santos, and then gave a reading at U. of the Redlands, then bar, country music, drunks, guys shooting pool.

Next day, tired and hung over, the drive to Irvine and Charles
Wright. After the reading my friend from Hawaii showed up. We go
to lunch and talk and talk. She drove me to the Orange County airport. I saw the statue of John Wayne. She said that she can find in
herself similarities to criminals, giving her a basis for judging what
they will do and whether they can be trusted in her business dealings, which she calls "agricultural economics," or growing and sell-
ing marijuana up and down the west coast, deliveries to private
homes from Seattle to San Diego. She talked about her betrayal of
her husband but said he mistreated her, gambled, and didn't come
home two or three nights a week. She'd have meals prepared and he
didn't show up. When he found out that she'd had an affair with
someone he knew, he hit the guy and fractured his jaw. She said he
got half an hour of pleasure out of it and will regret it the rest of his
life. She said she needs men all the time, prefers them to women, and
could never get married again, never give herself to one man. I said
maybe marriage doesn't work but it's sad that the ideal is unattain-
able, etc., and she said, "You're a romantic," and started coming on
with a mischievous tone. Told me other stories: she saw her lover
screwing her girlfriend in a jeep and was so upset she ran across a
field of sharp plants, tearing her feet; and her lover noticed and became angry, and started up his jeep suddenly, and her girlfriend's
head smashed into the roll bar causing trauma to the spine and a de-
generative bone problem. Also told me how her great love, after
leaving her for another woman, got herpes. Flying back to Oakland
I had such bad thoughts that I was afraid the plane would crash just
to punish me, but there must have been some nice, lucky people
aboard who saved us. Sartre says somewhere that a pretty woman on
board means the plane won't crash. A man with Parkinson's disease
was helped on board. Sartre would have been worried sick, probably demanded to be let off the plane. It almost seems to me that I
heard him say this in conversation, though I've only read his books.

July 31, '83

The movie *Jeanne Dielman* records three days in the life of a bourgeois woman who supports herself and her son through prostitu-
tion. Her few clients seem as bourgeois and proper as she is. They
look more doubtful than she is about her work. When she washes
dishes, the camera shows her washing every dish. When she leaves
the room, the camera continues to focus on the place she left, a sink
or a table, as if to suggest these objects are real in the same way that
she is. In the final scene she looks in the mirror and sees herself, no
longer sharing the ontological condition of an object like a sink or
a table. The suggestions of her breakdown are minimally given.
With no warning she stabs the client in her bed, and then stares into
the mirror with blood on her hand and blouse, stupefied and im-
mobilized. All her previous motion is revealed as a desperate effort
to maintain order and not to think about how she lives. Now that
she thinks about herself non-mechanically, she can't move. The
soul of the character is discovered to herself and to us. The movie
is without tricks or special effects, or fancy camera work, no
rhetoric, no lies. Every movie entails voyeurism more or less, but
this one has unusual purity. The story is absolutely serious and the
director is indifferent to the audience's sympathy or desire for entertainment. I was fascinated, never the least bored. Susan was also
fascinated and stayed to the end watching it with me, but John
walked out, making me doubtful—was the movie less good than I
thought? Then I read a good review in the *Village Voice* and felt surprised and pleased. I'm always surprised when a reviewer agrees
with me about a movie.

Aug. 1, '83

Inflicting pain on oneself to demonstrate one's state to another person, or making oneself ugly in order to reflect the ugliness one

sees in the other. Instead of striking at the other you ugly-up your-self in order to exhibit the effects of the other on yourself. Sylvia would become hysterical and make repulsive faces to show me what she feels I am. Reminiscent of an animal's threatening face, and maybe basic to all face-making even when it isn't conscious. The slightest change in expression communicates immensities. Philosophers worry about "other minds," and how one knows they exist. If only it were possible not to know.

Women are better actors than men because distinctions between the real and the unreal, the objective and the subjective, are less re-spected. This has become a value and a political issue in the sex wars.

Brenda returns from a meeting of her women's group and says, "Aristotle was wrong."

Oct. 4, '83
At 12:30 I met Vicki for lunch and we talked about her work. She is sane, perfectly balanced, and does everything well. No matter what I said about myself, it felt like a lie. At two o'clock I met the writing class, and was dopey and sleepy because of the gin and tonic at lunch. After class I went to the office and put my head on my arms on my desk and tried to snooze. Three students came by to talk about their term papers. I wasn't unreceptive but less than welcoming. I felt awful. About 4:30, I went home. After dinner, I went to the playground and played basketball alone, dribbling and shooting until it was too dark to see the hoop. I can move to my left and take running hooks, but only when playing against an imaginary opponent. There's a new idea of body control in the game. It has to do with stop-start motion, like break dancing. As in

dancing, your body can see itself or it can't. What the body sees determines how it moves and this describes the era. Today people move differently from the way they moved in the fifties.

Sandra says she wants to accumulate an archive on my literary career. I don't encourage or discourage her. I've had no career, only publications. I try to understand her desire to know me through my so-called career. It entails collecting reviews of my work. Why would she need them? I'm right in front of her.

Oct. 7, '83

Ear infection. Very deaf in the left ear despite antibiotics. I have no hope that it will get better. I won't ever hear well again, which means a huge loss of experience and a decline into abstraction and self. Less and less will call me to the world. I won't be able to go to plays or movies or make conversation at dinner parties. I'll misunderstand what people say, or fail to hear them. I'll seem rude or stupid or both. I won't hear the warning scream, the horn, or the raging engine, and I'll step into the path of the eighteen-wheeler or the whirring propeller blade. An Asian beauty will stop me in the street and beg me to tie her up and abuse her. I'll think she wants directions to the post office.

A sign in the hospital waiting room: "Don't leave the door open when you leave." A confusion of sound and sense. I can't say why exactly.

Prospect of trip to Washington, D.C., to work on Fulbright committee. Tedious work, and little freedom to do anything else I might enjoy except go to the Phillips gallery. Flying for hours, changing planes. Last time I sat up all night in my hotel room drinking bourbon and eating cold pills, and then my eardrum burst on the flight home. But I'm unable to say no; unable even to decide to say no, and then I think of all degrading things I haven't done, like kissing important literary asses—oh, maybe a few. I should be consistent, a good citizen. I get depressed when I haven't written anything for a long time, but I'll go to Washington. Maybe I'll see Laura. She'll talk about her troubles, and I mine.

Oct. 10, '83
Was threatened in my office again. First it was four tough-looking black kids who wanted money, but for some reason changed their minds and left without shooting me. Was it because I didn't get scared? Or because they noticed my signed photo of Shirley Chisholm. This time, the second time, it was a white kid. His face twisted. He could barely look me in the eye. His head angled to the right and he became hysterical and swept the papers and ashtray off my desk, shouting, "If I find out there's something going on, I'll cut your penis off and shove it down your mouth." He said "penis" instead of cock or dick as if that's the word you use in a university. He was intelligent, maybe felt guilty of excess. I said, "Nothing is going on and nothing happened." Nothing had, but I feel sick and disgusted and wish I could get out of here. Peter says call the campus cops. I will not. The kid read his wife's diary. It says nothing happened, but she talks about her feelings. That's more than enough, apparently. He must have been reading her diary for years, which is a crime much worse than the one she didn't commit.

Oct. 11, '83
Which is worse—living a lie consciously or unconsciously?

If you live a lie but it's not conscious, everything might be O.K. until the lie is revealed. Then things are much worse than they might have been if you hadn't been unconsciously living a lie. For example, the feeling of noble self-sacrifice in living for another, when revealed as self-serving, is horribly shameful. Marquis de Sade makes much of this.

In the sublimities of romantic feeling, sex isn't less animalish.

"My well of feelings undefiled," says Lord Byron. He abandoned his daughter in a convent, where she became ill and died, doubtless un-defiled.

Feb. 7, '84
Domestic daily life, he says, isn't worth giving up for the uncer-tainties of real life. The cost of a divorce is also forbidding, and he has no assurance, if he gets divorced, that he'll find anything better. Things would be just as bad or worse with another woman. Mainly, he wants assurance. He doesn't want to want. For some the unpre-dictable inspires fear. The predictable is what frightens me.

Feb. 8, '84
I don't have to remind myself that I want art, but so much pulls in the other direction. Then I think rhetoric or audience manipulation is a concession to life, since it answers to the most ordinary needs and sentimentalities. Maybe the worst writing is best in the eyes of God.

"It's hard to leave a marriage," I said. She said, "It's easy."

I've contributed to the local gossip about me. Now I want to go to a strange place where I have no friends and don't know anyone and can't speak the language. I've acquired a stalker who leaves flowers for me outside my front door and office door. She phones and makes silly conversation while her girlfriends giggle in the back-ground. It's very annoying and depressing. I'm sure I brought this upon myself simply by talking to people indiscreetly about my personal life.

Conversation:

> "Who can be happy with lies?"
> "Who can be happy with truth?"
> "A lie is repulsive to God."
> "When I hear it from Him, I'll believe it."
> "You're hearing it from me. Not good enough?"
> "No."
> "Maybe you should get some sleep. You're yawning."
> "Not because I'm bored, I assure you."

About this time, when my marriage was falling apart, Ethan and Jesse returned to Berkeley from Pittsburgh, where they had been living with their mother, and began living mainly with me.

May 16, '84

Tonight—having been expelled from Berkeley High—Jesse cleans up the kitchen after dinner. He's contrite, does a perfect job. Nothing like that ever happened in response to my pleas, arguments from love, gifts, the cajoling, or the rage followed by mawkish devotion. He said he was insecure at school. Carried books when he left the house, then sat in the park all day with the "burnouts." Now he wants to make an effort to redeem himself, and wants me to speak to his teachers. The psychologist at school said it's best if Jesse drops out and suffers the consequences of his behavior. Otherwise he won't know its value. I blame myself. It seemed, since I love him, I had to be doing the right thing. The psychotherapist, Albert Shapiro, advised me to stay out of it, let him hit bottom. Such advice relieves you of guilt associated with your kid in trouble.

Yesterday, an ex-convict—self-described—came to my office. He walks in, introduces himself, sits down, says he has a story. The creepy self-assurance of a psychopath. I didn't want to hear his story. I felt too uncomfortable, wanted him to go away but I listened. He assumed his story had commercial value, and stopped short of telling me everything. It had to do with atrocity photos and movies made by the Nazis, held by a certain person in Naples, for which people would pay any price. The interview was scary and ugly. I gave him names of agents in Los Angeles. He'd picked me to talk to because I teach a writing class. This is called community relations, I think, part of my job definition.

One feeling turns into another, sometimes its opposite. Sartre says nature oozes among indeterminate conditions. He hates nature, finds it nauseating, but chased young girls to the end of his life. Wallace Stevens, as opposed to Sartre, loves indeterminacies, what Sartre calls the "oozings." In "Motive for Metaphor," Stevens says, "You were happy in spring / With the half colors of quarter things," exactly the qualities that Sartre finds nauseating. The political differences between them were also extreme, basically physiological. Sartre had no poetry. Stevens had no sex; anyhow, not much, and didn't seem to like the sex he had.

A smell of something burning woke me up. I went to Jesse's room and accused him of smoking. He said no. I then found his water pipe and threw it out the window. I ordered him out of the house. He said, "Dad." I relented.

I would try to understand, but how does one try? Maybe I fear discovering something painful about my failure in regard to him. The women said I'm too protective, too approving of his wildness. To have to try to understand is discouraging. A situation that requires understanding already suggests failure of understanding; anyhow, confusion. Hard to understand that there are things to be understood. When I played ball, I didn't think, I moved, and it should be like that. I wish I could live like a peasant, close to land, close to the kids, and unafflicted by perversions of a society in decline.

May 21, '84

Editing jobs, readings, romances, domestic problems, book reviews, judging literary contests, traveling, phone calls, venereal disease, magazine articles, dinner parties, university classes, more classes, grocery shopping, fixing the plumbing, replacing a window, pruning the fig tree, doctors—my salvation, writing, I don't do. I hustle from thing to thing to thing, and never do what I want to do, and since I don't, I make sure that I can't. I think this self-reproachful way because I spent hours carving drawer handles, which are called "pulls." I used redwood molding. After many hours, I have assiduously accomplished nothing worth a damn. Tonight I'll go to the bookstore to hear the poet read from her new book. Her poems are about non-industrial countries where she has laid many revolutionaries as well as their oppressors.

June 8, '84

I've had two chairs upholstered and I worked for hours building bookcases. These actions confirm my immobility. Months have passed doing home improvement, a reinvestment in failure. I've heard that people remodel, add a deck or a room, or have the house painted just before they get divorced. Better to go to prostitutes for the affection they don't offer than live a secret life, as I do, compromised by love. Niven Bush said, "In the old days in Hollywood, screenwriters working together would send out for prostitutes the way they sent out for ham sandwiches. So they wouldn't risk falling in love." Do many people live a secret life? By definition the question can't be answered, but secret lives are probably less interesting than what you read in obituaries. Being secret, they're all the same. Your thoughts are secret, too. You try to express them fully, but there is always a residue. There's also unconscious thinking or feeling, which is secret from yourself. Sanity requires reservation, but revelation is critical to storytelling. The secret worm that flies in the night. Primo Levi says a writer cannot help but reveal himself in virtually every sentence. Montaigne says privacy or isolation breeds chimeras. Nietzsche says if you look into the abyss, the abyss will look into you. Pascal says if a man could sit still in his room, the world's troubles would end. He also says Jews were created by God to prove that not everything is indispensable. The son of God, Jewish, was dispensed with, after all. Pascal is a religious genius? I read him in French, in a seminar, in Berkeley, in 1959, with a British professor.

In journals you talk to yourself, but it's slow, not nearly as quick as thinking. The immediacy sought by writers, painters, and jazz musicians is achieved in photography. Photography wants to be art as achieved by writers, painters, jazz musicians.

The guy in Hollywood, whose name I can't remember, said, "I come home after work and say, 'Hi, honey, I'm back.' An hour ago I was hanging from a light bulb." He was two men in one body, each offended by the other. A monster of secret life. He wiped his palms unobtrusively on the sides of his trousers before he shook your hand. What if he felt no anxiety and didn't suffer? Wouldn't that be more monstrous? He went two or three times a week to a whorehouse. It cost a fortune, but when his wife spent too much he had a fit. She never spent a cent that wasn't justified. Driving home he smoked a Gaulois, a stinky cigarette, to cover the sex stench, and kept the car windows open. The highway fumes of Los Angeles would stick to his clothes and skin. A framed photo of his wife hung on the wall of his office. She looked youthful, radiant, sweet. He was proud of her. He adored her. He wanted a divorce. He said he worked in Hollywood because movies told the truth. They said what the world couldn't say to itself about marriage and everything else. Movies were a service to the human spirit. Without movies we lived in darkness. People say movies are dreams. He said we live in a dream. We go to movies for reality.

June 9, '84
Lilly's novel arrived. I read it in a few hours. I'm disturbed by the feelings her characters have—that is, kinds of feelings. I'm not like her characters. She writes extremely well but her characters have kinds of feelings, luxurious feelings. I tell myself they're widely shared, feelings people need and like to have. Social feelings. O.K. feelings. Without such feelings there would be no community.

Murders, rapes, muggings, violent movies, moronic television shows, and sports shows. A hundred million ordinary decent folks own handguns. "Sooner murder an infant in its cradle . . ." says Blake. Unless you hate your family, says Jesus, "you can't follow me." Religion and art deal with asocial forces, dark forces, as in the Abraham and Isaac story, or the Agamemnon and Iphigenia myth, or Grimm's fairy tales. Pilgrim cries, "Life, eternal life," as he flees his family.

She wants to be thin, not merely shallow, ignorant, unoriginal, uninteresting, etc.

I sit like a dullard afraid of saying something beyond redemption.

June 10, '84
The desire to see oneself as being in love, as if it were a condition of unalloyed good. Baudelaire says it's evil. Sartre says love ends in indifference, hatred, or perversions.

Memory: When I was a graduate student at Berkeley, I went to a party one night in the Berkeley hills at the home of a Hungarian countess, and I went home with a girl whom someone called "the perpetual runner-up to the Rose Bowl Queen." The gratuitous sneer was typical of the literary crowd, some of whom now write for television and movies. As for the girl, she did nothing to provoke the comment except to have blond hair and a nice body. I didn't see her again until months later. She was carrying her baby, waiting for a streetlight to change. She rested the baby on her right hip, which was thrust out slightly so the baby could straddle it. She let her weight fall on her left leg. I saw her from the back and was taken by how natural she looked, the relation of her useful hip and the line of her thigh in her jeans. It was good. It seemed beautiful rather than sexy, though I suppose the latter could be emphasized. (Isabella, for example, in the eyes of Angelo.)

July 21, '84
Took Jesse to Project Seed for his math class, and then to Dr. Saldinger. Jesse can do math, says his teacher, but seems to resist

learning and won't do homework. Saldinger says he isn't psychotic. Thus, the day began wonderfully, wonderfully.

My spiritual condition remains yes-no.

Oct. 23, '84

The psychotherapist–marriage counselor says that I abhor planning and seek risk because it's the way I receive confirmation of my right to live. For me things must happen by chance, because I need to feel that I have passed some test. It's as if I were a gambler. When Simone Weil says only the impersonal is holy, does she have this sort of thing in mind? When a psychotherapist has a love affair with a patient, a teacher with a student, a priest with a parishioner, or a boss with an employee, the sacredness of impersonality is violated.

Oct. 24, '84

My Sylvia memoir appeared in *Vanity Fair.* Beard called the same day. He was excited and he praised the piece effusively, then said, "But there was one word in it I didn't like." I ask what word. He says he can't remember. Does he do this deliberately or is it reflexive, a function of his character disorder? Maybe he's never had a feeling that wasn't about having a feeling. It's like what Mary McCarthy said of Lillian Hellman: "Every word is a lie, including 'if,' 'and,' and 'but.' " Beard gossips about me, says nasty things even to my friends, who repeat what he says, with some restraint, to me. Then comes the wild praise for the magazine piece. Of course he can't help poisoning it.

Nov. 27, '84

I talked about my altruism and the marriage counselor says, "In conventional psychoanalytic understanding, altruism is, at depth, rage and murderous feeling." I said I never feel those things, not even toward enemies. She says that I feel them unconsciously. To keep myself from acknowledging murderous inclinations or seeing the truth, then, I turn the feelings into altruism. What if I felt altruistic unconsciously? Only evil is repressed, I suppose.

Nov. 29, '84

Took Jesse to the Oakland airport and got a traffic ticket for a moving violation. I was in the left-turn lane and didn't turn left. Jesse was sick, and I was hurrying, depressed about his departure, and full of anxiety. During the time in Berkeley he seemed to decline. He arrived in high spirits and gradually sank into his sluggish dopey manner. I found matches in his room. He was smoking again. So many writers make dope glamorous; a form of romantic transgression, or world-weariness, or poetic sensitivity, or hipness. Mainly it's the stuff of ritualistic communion among inarticulate bores. With Jesse's old gang in Berkeley much happens that I'll never know. He takes drugs, dresses like a bum, and stays out all night. He spent the night before last and much of the next day with a girl in the back room. I was embarrassed and fled the house, though I didn't fail to notice she was very pretty.

Dec. 27, '84

Called Brenda. I tried to be pleasant. She was low-spirited. When I asked why she was low, she said, "That's how dense you are." I'm sad, too, but divorce is sad—all right, I'm dense. She told me she talked to one of my "friends" who said he met me in the street and I raved maniacally about my movie. That pissed me off. First of all, we're not really friends. We're friendly, that's all. Now that he characterizes me as raving about the movie, forget friendly. He makes me uncomfortable, so I rave. Everything we say is phony. When I run into him, I start raving about something. Otherwise, I have to pretend we can talk. Better to be a fool than phony. I rave when I'm uncomfortable, especially at dinner parties. If somebody is uncomfortable with me, I stay away. Hello and goodbye. Preferably neither; and I don't tell stories about the person. Distance is enough. More than that, something horrible might happen. He could get sick or have a fatal accident. I must be careful lest people are afflicted by my negative radiations. McGowan drowned, another is dead, another has a gruesome disease. It's not easy being so dangerous.

Jan. 29, '85

Sandra said her dentist had been in one of my classes years ago. I said, "What's her name?" Sandra told me. The face came to mind. A tall girl, half-Jewish, from Beverly Hills High. Sandra assumed we'd had an affair. Not true. The girl had had an affair with a junior colleague. I'd said to her, "He's married."

She said, "He's nice to me."

"So?"

"We took a bath together. I've never been naked with a man before."

Asked to review the man's work, I couldn't not think of him in the bathtub. While I waited to read my report to the tenured faculty, the pages trembled in my hands. I lost my breath as I read. I said his writing was graceful and empty, and students were fond of him. The two other reports were savage in their criticism. Afterward I went to Flanagan's office and said I want to read my report aloud to the man. I asked Flanagan to call him into the office. Flanagan said, "No." He wouldn't let me do what I didn't really want to do. Professor Bathtub got a job in another university. I've heard he's angry with me, the least of his detractors.

Sandra looked smugly amused, self-possessed, sitting in the way of a big-boned woman, her wide hips the house of herself. A superstar in molecular biology. If she were awakened in the middle of the night and asked how to run General Motors, she could tell them. A clear thinker, supremely rational despite a childhood with insane parents. She studied me through her glasses, a cool blue beam issuing from her eyes. "Would you like me to get you girls?" she said.

"Nice of you to ask, but no thanks."

"Would you like me to spank you?"

"I'm the professor."

"I'm the queen of kink. I'll do anything you dare say out loud."

Possible story: A well-known writer in his late seventies is asked to read the manuscript of a first novel by a young woman. He's afraid the manuscript won't be good, but he likes the woman and feels obliged to read it. If it's not good, he won't be able to lie to her. She can see that he is troubled by the prospect of reading her manuscript, but she pleads with him, tells him that she wants only to hear the truth, nothing else. He can save her years of futile dedication if he sees that she has no gift. He is swayed by her argument, and also by her violet eyes. He prays that her manuscript will seem good to him. After reading a few pages, he knows she has no imagination, no ear for language, no energy in her prose, and she has a common sensibility. She's not unintelligent but has no thoughts, just memories of experience. At best she's a kind of journalist, a purveyor of insipid middle-class emotions. Angry, he regrets reading the few pages. His feelings for the woman are seriously compromised, except for her eyes. He feels oddly depraved. It's a disaster. He is unable to finish reading her manuscript. Can't even look at it. He puts it out of sight.

Days pass and then the woman phones. She wants his opinion. He says he read only half of it. In fact, he read only about thirty pages, and it's well over six hundred pages long. He needs another week. They make an appointment to meet in a week. He doesn't look at the manuscript. The night before the appointment, he decides he must read it, but he can't find it and then remembers that he left it in the magazine rack, and the cleaning lady must have had it recycled with the newspapers. It's gone, irretrievable. After the opening thirty pages, maybe it improved, maybe it became good, even great. He dreads the meeting, the necessity of telling the woman the manuscript was so bad that he burned it. He'll demand to know why she thinks that she must be a writer. She will see Old Testament godlike rage.

Jan. 18, '86

At the beach cabin. Louisa asleep downstairs. I'm in the tower. It's a warm foggy night. I hear the ocean but can't see it. I've met local residents. Soon I'll have a post office box in town and receive mail there. I'll spend more and more time in the cabin, actually live here, though it's scary when it's stormy and the wind is loud, and the walls shake. From the tower I look out over the dunes and see where Jesse started a fire. I remember him leaping from behind a dune with the flames leaping behind him as he shouted, "Fire, fire," and came running to the cabin. I made him empty his pockets and found the matches. It was the second time he'd done it. He was six years old, Louisa's age. We had what some call a "problem."

Jan. 25, '86

I lost my glasses again, and missed lunch at the Faculty Club, and missed the reception. I can't remember whom the lunch or reception was for. Some visitor to the department? An important scholar? Must buy new registration tags for the car and renew my license. I forget everything. I'm surprised every day by something I've forgotten. I need the stability, the order, the domestic regime, but returning to married life has no appeal; and neither does loneliness.

Jan. 26, '86

Dinner with Brenda at Shin Shin. She said, "If you go nuts, I'll come to you. I'll put that in writing. Even if I have another family." I had to laugh, but her view of me is unnerving. I might have had a nervous breakdown now and then, but I'm perfectly O.K. otherwise. Marriage made us lonely. Both of us belonged to too many other people.

Jan. 28, '86

I forgot only one thing today, but I did renew my license and did get new registration tags, which I attached to the licence plate immediately and incorrectly.

Jan. 30, '86

Lunch with Adrienne. As we left the crowded restaurant, she said, "The trouble with this town is that it's full of creeps." I'm still laughing.

Feb. 1, '86

I should do what I do since I can't do otherwise.

Lunch with Virginia in San Francisco. She became a lawyer, got married, and has a comfortable life in Hillsborough. She has little time for conversation, but I listened to her when she was a student, and she felt that she owed me the same. She said, summing me up, that I'm a Mediterranean type, productive when married. As for Protestant individualism—making your own world—"There would be no satisfaction for you in that." I said, "I'm in the position you were in years ago when you used to come to my office in a chaotic state." She said, "And you were like the sea lions I saw while flying along the coast, up on the rocks, basking in the sun." She remembered Brenda sitting in the anteroom outside my office, legs crossed, her foot jerking and pointing toward the door. "Very proprietary," said Virginia.

Feb. 9, '86

Some of us continued to think of his first wife as his "real wife." Nobody said that to him, but he must have known what we thought and he may have thought the same. He accepted dinner invitations and made appointments to meet for a drink, but then he didn't show up. No excuses, no apologies. He let us think what we liked, and let us go.

The first time I saw Priscilla, she was in the Student Union cafeteria, sitting at a table with the Turk. A few days later the Turk invited me to a party. I figured she would be there. The apartment was full of dark men—Iranians, Pakistanis, Jordanians, Turks—and blond midwestern coeds. I felt like an honorary dark man. I'd been there only a moment when a door opened and a light from another room cut through the darkness and I spotted Priscilla. She was sitting on the Turk's lap on a couch. He was talking to another Turk. I crossed the room and sat beside them. The Turk was facing away from me, ignoring Priscilla. I said hello and asked her name. She told me and I told her my name and asked if I could phone her for a date. She said, "Yes," and told me her number. I didn't have to write it down. I asked her what she did and where she came from. All this while she was sitting on the Turk's lap. Minutes later, I left the party. I phoned her the next day. We made a date for dinner. I did the shopping and she cooked. I told her that I'd seen her in the Student Union cafeteria and I'd gone to the Turk's party only to meet her.

She said, "I've never been to the Student Union."

"If I hadn't seen you there, I wouldn't have gone to the Turk's party."

"You saw some other girl."

The marriage, the baby, the Ph.D., and the teaching job—everything began with a mistake. Not that it matters. The most careful and accurate understanding might have led to worse. In no time Priscilla was pregnant. We went to a justice of the peace in the country. He married us in the living room of his house and said, "You done good."

May 10, '86
The Wife of Bath talks about the "wo that is in marriage." From that wo came the *Iliad* and ten thousand novels.

May 25, '86
I told Jeremy about the girl hitching a ride in Malibu, how she loosened her hair, tossed it free, and put up her thumb and got a ride almost instantly. Jeremy then told me that he was on a roof with a woman who wore her hair pulled back tightly and held by a rubber band. He plucked the band free, and dropped it off the roof. The woman's hair fell about her shoulders, but she didn't behave like a woman with loosened hair. She went down seven flights of stairs and retrieved the rubber band. I loved the story and asked him if I could have it.

I introduced Jeremy to Cassandra and told him that she'd won a prize for her book of poems, and was in the running for a Pulitzer. He said, "Congratulations," and then asked her questions about her poetry, and said he was going to buy her book. When she walked away, Jeremy said, "Nice ass." He then shrugged and added, "That's how I judge poetry." She'd had thoughts along the same line. When she won the prize, Cassandra said, "The judges didn't see me, you know."

May 26, '86

I asked the students: "If Saint Augustine and Rousseau were coming down Telegraph Avenue, which of them would you like to meet?" The Indian girl said Saint Augustine. The others picked Rousseau. They're likable, optimistic, mass-entertainment white kids from families with a median income of seventy-five thousand dollars a year. In the voice of the Indian girl I heard something traditional and ancient, like soul. After class, she came up and asked, "Do you know my name?" There were over twenty students in the class, but I must have felt guilty for favoring her too much. I'd repressed her name. I didn't want to know it. I apologized. She told me her name. I forgot it immediately as we shook hands. How could she tell that I didn't know her name? I gave her papers the highest grades. I called on her immediately when she raised her hand. She'd seen a blankness in my eyes. The particular recognition, the love, was absent.

May 30, '86

Memory: My mother would take me to Klein's, a cut-rate department store on Union Square. She held my hand, afraid I'd get lost or kidnapped in the confusion of the narrow aisles where hundreds of mothers bent over bins full of shirts, sweaters, jackets, sneakers, and underwear. From the bins mothers plucked a bargain. My mother plucked a pair of greenish corduroy pants for me. The material brushed between my thighs and whistled. I whistled in the morning as I walked to school, whistled in the afternoon walking home. I despised those pants. My mother said, "What's wrong with them?"

"The color."

"What's wrong with the color?"

"Looks like vomit."

"Nobody in the family is so picky. I don't know where you come from. The pants cost only two dollars."

I wore the green cordoruy pants when I played stickball. I remember the feel of the stick in my fists and my heart beating with
anticipation as I waited for the pitch, and then seeing the pitch. I
swung and caught the ball in the middle of the stick and there was
a speedy blur soaring over third base. I took off running. Above the
rage of traffic and my team screaming for me to run, I heard my
shoes slapping the asphalt and my green pants whistling to first,
whistling to second, whistling to third, whistling home. That's my
life—good hit, horrible pants.

Sept. 30, '86
Geiger came to my office. I'd given him a B on his paper. It was badly
typed, food-stained, and passages were illegible. He said softly, as if
he were too hurt to raise his voice, "You know I'm very intelligent."

I said, "You'll probably get an A in the class. Let's talk about
something important."

Now he was angry. I was angry, too. He wants me to give him
a low grade so he can feel injured. A destructive intimacy exists between us, which belongs in a European novel, not to life in Berkeley. The repulsive condition of his papers, indeed. He provokes me,
makes war because there is no word for what he wants. I refuse to
go to war. The weather is too pleasant. I'll give him an A and we'll
pass each other on campus without saying hello. Our eyes won't
meet. If he walks into the men's room and sees me pissing, he'll
back out. When he needs a letter of recommendation for law
school, he won't ask me. Years from now, I'll hear that he's in serious trouble, but I'll have given him an A. I can't be blamed.

Feb. 24, '87
Watching a TV drama with Louisa about an old married couple
who enjoy a nostalgic communion, remembering the love they
once felt for each other, and they fall in love again. Louisa says,

"How could they do that unless they got divorced? I mean aren't they already in love if they're married?" If I knew how to tell her about adult reality, I would, but I can't even write about it in a way acceptable to adults.

April 11, '87

I go away and find myself thinking about the problems I think about at home. Then time passes and, little by little, I notice that the hours feel natural rather than psychological. The day goes from light to dark, rather than from anguish to anguish, and I'm being taken out of myself by the beauty of the place and I'm happy until I remember that I must make a phone call. Talking to Priscilla the subject is always money, but while talking about money I realize that I miss her voice. After hanging up, I turn on the radio. Loud.

A woman told me that she was suffering with a mysterious condition. She had swollen glands, throat lesions or thrush, and was extremely tired and weak. Her doctor couldn't name the disease, but it seemed she was describing HIV. She said she hadn't been intimate with anyone for years, except me. She'd just begun living with a man, but he tested negative. Despite her symptoms her doctor refused to think that she, an all-American young mother, might have the disease. He'd tested her for everything but HIV, as if in the hope that something less terrible would be discovered. I assumed the worst.

May 10, '87

Wish I were better than I am, and not afraid of dying.

Thought of the loneliness in dying and then of the Kurdish tribes-men outside the tent of one who is sick and in pain. When he moans, all of them begin moaning.

Lack of self-respect is a reason for the mistreatment of others. It can also be a reason for treating others like royalty. In sex you can flip-flop from day to day.

Bought sneakers for Jesse, white Converse hightops. Went to the office and read Yiddish poetry. I think I've lost my favorite pen. Is it a sacrifice? Magical notions arise from the fear of death. The campanile bell, one dull gong. One A.M. It sounds ominous.

Courage is continuing to perform your daily tasks, and being hopeful despite the odds, not inflicting your fears on others, and remaining sensitive to their needs and expectations, and also not supposing, because you're dying, nothing matters any longer. Best is quietly to die.

May 13, '87
Talked to Allen Graubard twice this morning. He listened without comment. He seemed flat, not happy, not interested. Has his own problems. No dramatic value in talking about how you thought you were going to die if you don't.

June 10, '87
She was dying, yet weirdly exhilarated, fearless, transported by morbid sublimity while undergoing test after test for everything but HIV. Then, at my insistence, she tested for HIV. She was negative. So what did she have? The blues? And why now do I feel this lack of heart? Am I not convinced that I'm free of danger? The fear was too intense too long. Something in me changed permanently is how it seems. I continue to watch myself for symptoms, continue to wonder about hers. I urged her to go away, go home to the

southern California sun, be with her parents and kid. She said she wanted to go, but her ex-husband advised against it. He is remarrying. If she appears it will be confusing for their son. I said it won't confuse, it will clarify. Just go. Don't discuss it. She said, "I could," and then, "I will." Her going seemed necessary, as if she'd take the disease with her. She'd get better down south in the sunshine. She was sanguine, not happy, feeling safe and free, a tragic heroine who survived. She'd been too weak to climb a flight of steps, and had swollen lymph nodes, general debilitation, weight loss. She told me her father once had to come save her from a man she was living with in North Dakota. Her father drove out there, then drove home with her. She'd sensed happiness in him, driving back to California. A woman in distress is the most powerful motivating force. I heard a line like that in the movie *The Razor's Edge.* Never read the novel.

June 14, '87
Went to a party at the home of Adrienne's friend. A man dying of AIDS read poems. One was about his pleasure in conviviality. He said he was grateful to have had one day of it, but wanted another and another, and then talked about his fear of the uncertain future and nothingness. The invitation to the party had been written in a silly, lighthearted way. The poetry reading was simple, not rhetorical. All very civilized and good-spirited. In the kitchen I saw a blondish-red-haired man fondling a younger dark man, fingering the waistband of his pants, staring into his eyes, smiling with a confident knowing gleam as the younger man tried nervously to talk. AIDS isn't the end of sex. Franny said that in the hospital where she works, in the AIDS ward, there are lots of sexual goings-on. She found it shocking, but then said, "Sex is life."

Old as life. RNA-DNA. Natural cell chemistry. A cure is unnatural.

Somebody tells a story and I see images, and enjoy the drama. But there are people who take the dramatic value out of stories. For example: "We were trekking across Siberia in the middle of winter, followed by wolves, and our food was almost gone. I was wearing my gray sweat socks, the ones I bought in Albany."

I don't want to sleep. Too vigilant. I fear the fear. What to do? Maybe I should sell the house. It's small and surrounded by wild vegetation, the least expensive house in Kensington, but still a tremendous luxury. Nobody should live in a house he actually loves. All I need is a room in someone's garage.

June 15, '87
TV news show. San Mateo. A photo exhibit of AIDS people. One of them, a young woman who contracted the virus through intravenous drug use, was questioned in the typical, brutally stupid way about how she feels. "Tired. It's scary," she said. The camera was gone instantly, focused on something else, as if her answer had met cruel indifference. She probably said a few more words that made her condition seem unpleasantly painful, or started crying. "It's scary." What a child would say. She was a child. The sick are children.

I told Brenda about my fear. She said now she'd have to tell her "support group." I didn't get it—she needs support? Was she serious? Seconds passed before I laughed. The remark was funny no matter what she intended.

Day after day I go to sleep afraid to go to sleep. My only work is physical labor. Long good day in the backyard digging out a rectangle for the brick patio. Matt bought yellow bricks, too shiny for the house. I wanted old bricks, but Matt is a strong-minded guy. I'll learn how to do it myself and use old bricks elsewhere. In brief, I'm paying Matt to build a patio that he likes, made of new yellow bricks that I dislike.

Went to dinner at Siam with Allen, then Black Oak Books to say hello to Mona Simpson after her reading. She said she's at the Jerassi Foundation. She was signing books. Couldn't talk. Went home and telephoned David, Liz, Tom, and Katya, then tried to sleep. I talk to friends just to hear their voices.

The fear of disease guarantees good behavior. A quiet small life is a fine thing.

Talked to Allen about Wittgenstein, told him I could repeat what I've read, but I don't really get it. He quoted Wittgenstein's remark that philosophical problems are "language on vacation," and said he dissolves, not resolves, problems. Oh.

Phone has rung repeatedly for the past several days with nobody at the other end.

There was nobody else I could talk to, so I talked to her and had to assume that I was talking—through her—to many others. Then I always forget and I tell her stuff too good to keep to herself. I regret it afterward. In the moment, I forget my suspicions and even my anger, as if I don't fully believe in what I feel.

June 16, '87
After a dozen or so trips, I couldn't carry another sack of concrete up the hill. I felt as if my back and heart would give out. Matt can do it all day. He said he was going to the weight room at the gym after work. He's in his twenties. I'm in my fifties. I smoke, drink, and

don't sleep well, but I felt embarrassed at having to quit. The pick and shovel undid me before the carrying began. Matt said to save myself for tomorrow. To understand physical labor you have to do it—continuous strain until the job is done, unlike workouts in a gym, a certain number of lifts and presses, etc. A different kind of strength, too.

A virus doesn't live, doesn't die. It enters the host, and without desire or intention, uses living cells to reproduce itself. A molecular structure "uses." Very like a critic, reducing the host to a reproduction of itself, the critic.

Slava came by, smoked and drank, and seemed anxious. I said, "You're afraid if you leave your marriage, you will discover the problem was in you, not the marriage, and then feel as bad as now, if not worse." He said, "Exactly right." Could that be right? I said only what I'd thought before my divorces.

Reading Sartre. He hates the bourgeoisie. Hates inauthenticity and discovers it everywhere. Admires self-destructive figures. They must be authentic. Thinks it is difficult to be what one is, a concern reminiscent of the Hasidic tale of Rabbi Meir. He worries about what he will say if the Lord asks, "Meir, why did you not become Meir?" Amidst Sartre's verbal deluge, he sometimes questions his feelings: A moment of joy makes him wonder if it's authentic, O.K. to feel it. He respects workers. They have sincere relations, unlike the bourgeoisie; Virginia Woolf felt similarly about peasants. Me, too, though it's sentimental.

The mystery caller again. Every day at different hours. Long silence on the answering machine. It was him or her.

June 18, '87

At dinner with Fred and Elaine. Fred talked about Brazil. Elaine talked about *The Untouchables,* telling the whole movie, said its stylized gore was a way of giving the audience what it wants to see—murder—without suffering moral doubts. From the ancient Greek tragedies to Hollywood, style is the sign of art. I tried to make that point in my essay on murder as the central theme of modern literature. I failed. I could come up with examples in Nabokov, Bellow, Mailer, Sartre, and others where murder is explicitly and self-consciously the subject and the dramatic action, but then couldn't say what had to be said. "The Nazis proved that murder is feasible," says Isaac Rosenfeld, more or less. "Feasible" is the word, the extraordinary word.

Working with Matt and Jesse. The concrete slab for the patio was laid, embedded with steel. It will survive earthquakes and last much longer than me. After dinner I fell asleep, and then woke at one A.M., and then went shopping at the all-night Safeway. Louisa comes tomorrow.

4:45 A.M. Can't sleep. Thinking of Jake, the way he talks over me, in the Berkeley manner, raising his voice to suppress what I'm about to say, especially on the phone, and he answers questions before I finish asking, reflexively, as if he were responding to an order, proving himself, exceeding requirements of conversation, or he shouts me down as if he will be caught at something if he allows me to finish saying what I have in mind, and wants to distract me from saying it. I can't find the image to suggest what he is like—extremely eager, over-responsive. Maybe I make him nervous. He asks how I am, then says how he is before I can answer, then abruptly changes the subject.

———————

I think of ruined friendships, and review the reasons why things went bad. Something I said that didn't have to be said. Excitement made me stupid with feeling. I spoke thoughtlessly, or imprecisely, and then there was no way to explain, no way to be forgiven.

I smoke. If I develop a cough I'll be able to suppose it's because I smoke, and I won't worry about the disease.

June 19, '87

Events don't matter if it makes no difference if the events never happened. Like most sexual experience, maybe. But most of life seems "as if" until the terror, the end of "as if." Apparently I was waiting for reality to arrive. I thought I could do this and that, or do nothing, and let time go by, but then comes the end of "as if" when there is nothing but necessity.

I go to a reading given by a famous writer. The work being read isn't good, but there is a large admiring crowd and they're wildly enthusiastic. Their enjoyment makes all writing seem stupid. I'd spent most of the day with a pick and shovel in my backyard. I was unshaven, wearing dirty jeans, and must have looked like an old Berkeley type who, in his loneliness, wandered off the street into the bookstore to be among people.

Louisa said she'd been urged to talk to me about the divorce, and said Naomi Schwartz told her about her sad childhood as the daughter of divorced parents. Louisa can walk from her mom's house to mine in about two minutes. She comes to me anytime she or her mother wants, and has a key to the house, and a bedroom. There is nobody she competes with for my affection. She's better off than children of married parents. The only time I was ever annoyed at her was when she'd gone to church with her mother and then came here and started babbling to me, an old Jew, about Jesus. I hustled her out the door and back to her mother. Louisa isn't sad. Do they want her to be sad?

I'm not confrontational. I prefer passivity, indifference, obliviousness. I want less and less to do with more and more.

While wearing my glasses, I turn off the light, and the darkness seems larger, fuller, closer, not simply an opaque blot but a version of light.

Very late. I don't want to sleep. I want another sip of bourbon, another cigarette. I watch TV and a summary of the day's baseball games begins with brief clips of moments in the action. I'm impressed by how it's all right to watch these moments. It's life, I think, and anything that is life, however ordinary and insipid, is all right. Baseball makes this apparent more than other games because it isn't divided up by halves or quarters or minutes. Since it's not controlled by time, baseball is time. The main thing is life, which is a certain amount of time, and there isn't much more to have or to want or to enjoy.

June 23, '87

At the benefit dinner for people with AIDS, Shirley MacLaine gave a talk in which she said the epidemic is our chance to show love and to become closer to the beyond, and to understand death. It was an opportunity to experience something not otherwise available and to learn. Ran into Chris R. later at the organic chicken store. She said she had been offended and appalled. Said MacLaine wanted us to get AIDS. When I got home, Maylie Scott phoned. Wants to use my beach cabin for a weekend with somebody dying of AIDS.

June 24, '87

Had the shakes very bad, like epilepsy, but it came in waves, convulsive, and also a fever. I was terribly cold and it was impossible to warm myself though I lay under the comforter and three blankets. Finally, I fell asleep. I needed another body beside me. This strange illness first happened to me years ago when I was a graduate student at Berkeley. I went from O.K., even good, to convulsions with the terrible coldness. It has happened again about ten times since then. Maybe it's a kind of sunstroke combined with a virus. Lots of sun and liquor yesterday, and not much work. Now I'm confused about the days, but remember dinner with Masao. He raved more than I did, and is more committed to extremes as he grows older. He said Khaddafy isn't more crazy than Reagan, and the Arabs ought to have the atomic bomb. There was also a long serious phone call from Frank. He said he tested negative, and has become an expert on the disease. He explained the retrovirus to me, telling me about its peculiar enzyme that facilitates its reproduction. He said there are drugs that inhibit the enzyme, and then said you last fifty-three weeks, and it's not quality time. Last night, during my fever and shakes, it came to me that one's blood could be entirely drained and heated and then returned to your system with all the viruses killed. I thought of waking Louisa and asking her to help me, but didn't want to frighten her. I was shaking so badly that I had trouble turning on the lights and getting blankets out of the closet.

Bought a post-hole digger and dug three holes alongside the patio for the retaining wall.

No way to stay clean except to do your work and not answer the telephone.

"They come, they go, they sing, they dance; of death no news."

There is nothing to prove. There is only the day, the time, the effort to say some necessary thing. Writing now seems like an insane self-sacrifice. I say this from established comfort at least partly due to writing.

Worked at post holes, shopped, cooked dinner, and called Fred to ask about his bone scan. No cancer.

Louisa said she is now "used to" me and should stay with me.

Personalities are what they are, like different kinds of trees, and we're all predictable after the fact. "That's just like so-and-so," we say. True, but we'd never have predicted it before the fact.

June 28, '87
Dinner with Ethan. He says the Toyota needs transmission work, about $500, and he would do it himself if he had a place to work and tools. While he was here the phone rang, demanding my head. Couldn't say a proper goodbye to Ethan.

Reading Gauguin's *Noa Noa* at a table outside the French Hotel. In 1898, he thought Tahiti had already been spoiled. Could he see it now, he'd know the meaning of spoiled.

After dinner with Ethan I went to see *Full Metal Jacket*. I'd go to any Kubrick movie. It was gruesomely violent, overwrought—intense sensational drama and, simultaneously, cold, distanced, resistant to feeling. Shocks are allowed, and no meaning, and no real characters beyond a fat kid in boot camp who kills himself. The movie is extremely immediate. It says now, now, now. Afterward nothing. Characters are brutally killed, but most important is the visual impact. The fat kid commits suicide and the next scene is a luridly sexual event in Vietnam. The movie, in its stylistic essence, is what we are.

I sleep on a futon on the floor. The bed is too luxurious, though not a good bed.

She phoned, said she liked my essay, but I didn't let myself feel pleasure in being praised, lest I relax and become incautious. Must constantly remind myself, while talking to her, that I am talking—through her—to many others since she won't or can't keep anything to herself. Talking to her is like making a speech, addressing thousands, or performing a political act since I never know how things I say will be repeated. There is no way to talk to her alone; that is, absolutely no way for me to talk only to her. Everything is repeated in her letters, phone calls, and conversations around America and the western world. It's hardly ever this way with men friends, not even with those who are basically female and thrive on exposure and gossipy revelations. Semi-naked girls in magazines and movies are emblematic. Henry James was once considered obscene for psychological revelations. A twenty-four-hour-a-day gossip program on radio would have millions upon millions of listeners. Aside from the inherently evil kick, would anyone find this kind of thing fascinating?

Had to buy four eighty-pound sacks of concrete, then carry them up the hill for the posts of the retaining wall. First I decide to carry only one sack a day, but then find myself doing all four in an hour, giving myself five minutes rest between sacks. Each trip after the first seems more dreadful than the last, even going back down the hill without a sack is dreadful, and then just seeing the sack is dreadful, then finding the will to lift it, and then the strength, then then then the climb, every step another degree of torture. There is no plateau of pain. It gets worse and worse until I set the sack down.

July 1, '87

Another threatening letter from the divorce lawyer with more claims for "arrearages," which sounds like anal intercourse. I've given more than legally required already, but I must keep on giving and I musn't complain. No price is too great for freedom. No matter how much I'm obliged to give I'm far from the place where I'd been for so long. It's true that I'm miserable, but in a different way.

If I could know what another person imagines I'm saying as I say it, I might hear myself for the first time and know for certain if I were insane.

A close-up photo of a dying person makes you feel your own mortality, the ultimate alienation of you from yourself.

He talks in a way that suggests he's said these things before, told this story before, built toward this punch line before. He bursts into performance during conversations, as if unable to bear the natural flow since he fears it might not include him every single minute. He gets louder and louder, shouting down all others, and laughing at his own jokes.

A man's lover becomes furious when he refuses to invite her into his house for a cup of tea and chance to meet his wife.

The Couple: She wants whatever he says he doesn't want, and she doesn't want whatever he says he wants. The moment she knows what he dislikes, she likes it, and she dislikes what he likes. This is true in everything from friends to movies to politics to sex. She takes a position opposite to him in every possible way. She is a square, which is why he fell in love with her. She was rational, judicious, reserved, reliable, honorable. When she saw what he loved about her, she began to talk hip and adopt radical attitudes. She picked up hitchhikers, wandered in dangerous places, and fantasized about adultery and lesbianism.

I saw the agitator on television. He is a politician, not a leader. He has ideas, but no charisma. He is on the right side of things, and yet seems like a sleazy operator. Maybe he has no sense of self, no subjectivity, and feels as if something is missing, so he becomes an agitator, as if he could fill his interior emptiness by stirring up the world.

I asked the police to get a record of phone numbers from which calls were made to my number. They couldn't. It would violate the privacy of the person who had violated my privacy. But if I gave the police a particular phone number from which I suspected the calls might have come, they would tell me yes or no. I knew what number to give them, but it made me a little sick thinking about it. I didn't want them to tell me yes or no. I wanted them to show me a list. If I happened to spot the number, it would be a surprise, not a confirmation of a low suspicion. If the suspected person turned out to be guilty, I'd feel responsible.

Toward the end of the eighties, I lived alone except when my daughter visited. I had a girlfriend, and went out a lot and was unusually social.

Jan. 28, '89

The pressures of Berkeley became unbearable. I needed a quiet place and decided to go to the cabin. But then the other me asserted himself. I phoned her and asked her if she wanted to go to the cabin with me. She said she had too much to do. I tried to convince her to come with me. She was firm, she had too much to do. I left town alone. At the cabin, alone and writing, it was good until the phone rang. It was her. She said with no preface, "If you wanted to be with me, you wouldn't have gone to the cabin." Now I'm too upset to work. When I have my writing, I have something. It means only that I haven't given away all that I have. I am sinful in this small remaining possession. I must not have anything, neither property nor time, nor writing, and I must not want privacy. Then I would be perfect and I would have the opportunity to give still more. There is hardly any difference between a love affair and religious worship. What comes to mind are American cults where sad little people give away everything they have.

Feb. 4, '89

I write about society's blindness to how it lives, but it's crucial to my writing that I refuse to see what I'm saying—at least not until it's said. There is a distance between me and everything I write. When I try to see what others see in it, I find myself blinded by what I intended and its relation to what emerged. Primo Levi thinks writing is inevitably a personal revelation.

Feb. 6, '89

After the dinner party, standing at the door and about to leave, saying thanks and goodnight, there always seem to be a few thousand last words that didn't get said during the evening. This conversation at the door, this apparent unwillingness to leave—as if to leave is a repudiation of love, a bitter concession to reality.

Feb. 14, '89

I spent so much money this week that I don't even dare think about it. My problem is being unable to think about my problems. I am intimidated by the prospect of a confrontation with the unthinkable. Like smoking—just to think about the need to stop smoking makes me smoke.

Feb. 23, '89

Martinez courthouse to file divorce papers. The clerk says, "Who told you to come here? You don't have all your papers. Go back to your lawyer." I turned to go and saw, standing behind me, a Mexican woman. She could barely speak English, but managed to explain to the clerk that she couldn't afford a lawyer and was trying to do the paperwork herself in order to divorce her husband, Modesto, who wasn't in the States, and who wasn't necessarily going to sign the papers if she managed to send them to him—she didn't know his address—and Modesto might not even want the divorce. She had a child with her, a dark little being with Indian features. I wanted to help her, but I couldn't even help myself and started walking away and would probably have gone home, but just then Tatiana Sundquist happened by on some legal business and she saw me and realized instantly—in my posture and expression, not from anything I said—that I was at a loss. She snatched the papers out of my hand, barely glanced at them, filled them out correctly in a flash, then led me back to the clerk and took me to the front of a line of about ten lawyers wearing suits and ties, and said something to them about why I had to go first. I didn't catch what she said, but they didn't argue with her, and then she rushed away, having changed the course of my life, not to mention the lives of several people connected to me. I could tell that, in her hurry to go, she forgot everything that just happened even before she left the room.

March 22, '89
We're divorced. I don't feel any different, but of course Brenda lives up the hill less than a minute away if I drive, and Louisa comes by frequently and stays with me. It's nice. I have a little house surrounded by trees, and I have a good-looking girlfriend whose husband lives in Europe. It makes me feel like a communist. I want the whole world to live this way.

April 11, '89
Life in the middle class requires constant vigilance since you have things which inspire lust in others. Not only for your material things. When I told Albert, my psychotherapist, that I know a lot of people and when I drive across the country I never have to stay in a motel, he said, "How do you suppose that makes me feel?" Whatever he intended, the question left me feeling unbalanced.

May 29, '89
At Slava's party he introduced me to a German scientist. A woman came up beside the scientist. He said, "This is my wife." I believed he was absolutely correct.

Mary Gaitskill phoned. I said, "You sound tired." She said, "I always sound tired." I find myself laughing, then remembering how funny she can be.

———

Florence shows up wearing a very short miniskirt. She notices Katya staring and says, "Do you think I look ridiculous?" Katya says, "As opposed to what?"

May 31, '89

Met Katya for ice cream. We sat and talked. She said the markings on a sparrow's head give it a look of intense concentration. That's true. I'd noticed it myself, but never thought to remark on it.

June 9, '89

Katya says her girlfriend let herself be picked up by a man who "is inferior in education and brains." I start laughing at her expression. She continues, "I mean he didn't go to good schools, but I suppose he showers regularly." In brief, her girlfriend was picked up in the street and went home with the man. "He can mean little to her," says Katya, but the interesting thing is that her girlfriend "worries about whether he really cares for her. She insists always on paying for herself, and then she worries if she isn't less expensive than a prostitute." Katya never jokes, yet manages quietly—and as if unintentionally—to be amusing. She talks about absurdities in the lives of her friends, relatives, lovers, and professors. She understands everything I say, even when I'm incoherent and not too sure what I said or even wanted to say. I'd never talk to a man the way I talk to her, but of course men are genetically programmed to kill one another.

Katya says the man is Italian, a chef in a restaurant in Monterey. His name is Donny. Did her girlfriend spend a night with him? I asked. Katya said, "Two weeks. It took two weeks before she began to realize that she had to go home." Her girlfriend says, "Donny is model gorgeous," and she was happy during the two weeks, though he is unworthy of her. He's nice enough, but she "can't talk to him, and the sex isn't finally enough. It's only pleasure." Besides, she didn't want to fall in love with him. They can't get through dinner before Donny is around the table tearing at her underpants. Two weeks of that is enough.

Lewis, a businessman, plenty brainy but hooked on cocaine, foulmouthed and irresponsible, not returning phone calls, losing important documents. I believed he had no taste until the dinner at his house and I saw his collection of orientalia, especially the rugs. I admit I was resentful. It was unfair—a guy like him shouldn't have those rugs and porcelains. No books. His record collection is "semi-classical" music. His paintings are upscale restaurant art. Lots of muted color relations, blurry shapes. Empty L.A. chic. Those paintings shouldn't be in the same room with the rugs. Lewis bought these rugs. How could he have bought the paintings? A lapse in judgment? No. A single principle operates. He's post-modern fashion conscious, thinks empty is a form of good. He bought the porcelain, maybe, as a hedge against the worthless paintings.

"Language is a woman. Her mode is to be used, her truth betrayal." Katya cried when I repeated it. She thinks I've been hurt beyond recovery, made cynical.

Katya talked about her suicidal friend; said he'd been low for weeks. When she told him that he looked better lately, he became annoyed.

I press the phone receiver so hard against my ear that it begins to hurt. Small discomforts increase. The increasing strain, moment to moment, of an ordinary day, and the increasing value of ordinary, undramatic experience—like working about the house, a conversation with the wine merchant. No more wild stuff, what I used to do, then do again and again, as if something different might happen. It never happened. I don't feel bored with company, but anxious about time I spend away from myself. Being alone seems too luxurious. Another anxiety sets in. When the phone rings, I become hopeful that I'm about to be saved from myself.

Katya agreed to have lunch with a guy she doesn't like, but found at lunch she liked him, and then figured it was because he was at such a disadvantage. Nobody would tell me anything like that except Katya. She makes something of moments that nobody else would consider worth thinking about.

Heard Joe Williams sing at Yoshi's. He was exceptionally fine, and I wondered how his gift seems to him. When he is singing, he looks almost amused at how good he sounds. He had a full house. The crowd was very pleased. I drove home a little drunk, and went much too fast down Oxford Street. I was frightened after the fact, thinking about the dark houses rushing by. It's more frightening when I come home late from San Francisco with no memory of the drive. Lying in bed at three A.M., I try to remember how I got here. I must have driven along Army Street and then across the Bay Bridge, but I remember only the music at Cesar's and people dancing.

June 17, '89

No woman. A sense of odd detachment—detached from attachment. This wonderful time alone is given to me. I couldn't have taken it, couldn't have had this by my own will to have it. I phoned Katya and was surprised at my pleasure in hearing her voice. So much for the wonderful time alone. She said she'd been reading my essays and expected them to be pale. Instead they were dark. Such feeling, she thinks, should be reserved for religious experience. I nothing protest.

The material thing closest to a pure idea is money. If a pair of shoes and a pair of binoculars both cost three hundred dollars, they become three-hundred-dollar entities. Money is anti-matter. It dematerializes the world. The idea is put differently by Marx and Engels. Mathematicians talk about mathematical objects, which are immaterial but objects nonetheless.

I was in L.A., walking down Wilshire Boulevard with Louisa, then three years old. She was wearing a multicolored sweater that her grandmother had knit for her. A woman said, "How much do you want for that sweater?" Louisa told everyone about it, laughing, as if it were funny that a stranger wanted to buy the sweater off her back. Cold cash is never colder than in L.A.

The Couple: She says she dropped a number of friends because her husband dropped them. After the divorce she worked to redeem the friendships. Now she feels bewildered—how could she have behaved like that? With terrific resentment, surprising to herself, she blames her behavior on her former husband. I did the same thing and found myself no less resentful toward my ex-wife, and bewildered by my behavior.

The Couple: There was a period when he wanted to return to his family, but he was advised against it by doctors, psychotherapists, and friends—what he called "society." Everyone told him the same thing—to learn how to take care of himself—but almost immediately he was being taken care of by a new woman. It made no difference that his wife, in everyone's opinion, was smarter, more sophisticated, better-looking, and more appropriate to him than the new woman, who had a serious speech defect and amblyopia. It didn't even make any difference that he agreed with everyone about his wife, and it made no difference that he'd have done anything to get free of the new woman, except actually get free of her. He said to me, "I'd give my right arm." He feels guilty about the divorce, I think. As a form of self-punishment, he became attached to the new woman. She holds her head in an oddly tilted way because she's deaf in one ear. Neither he nor anyone else imagines she is the reason for his divorce—that is, he couldn't have left his wife for her. Maybe he hated his wife. Maybe the new woman is a strange expression of hatred.

The Couple: Dying, he refused to let his ex-wife visit though she'd been able to make him well in the past. It would be like forgiving her if she were allowed to make him well. He preferred to die. Can't touch wounded animals.

A memory: Arthur Kleinman, a furrier, union member, reader of the *Times,* heavy smoker, and regular in the Garden cafeteria next door to the *Forward* building, stepped outside after eating his whitefish sandwich and drinking a cup of coffee, and, as he'd done thousands of times, started to walk home, when he had a heart attack and died in the street. A sandwich, a cup of coffee, the *Times,* a cigarette—almost all the significant pleasures of life—and he starts walking home . . . Next thing anyone knows is that Lynn Nations from Abilene, Texas, who is Arthur's wife, is trying to throw herself off the balcony of our apartment on the fourteenth floor in the Seward Park building. We'd been neighbors for many years. I was in her apartment almost every day, a kid who didn't speak English, so Arthur would speak to me in Yiddish, and Lynn would tease me. "Arthur, did you hear what he called the telephone wire? He called it a *shtrich."* They would smile with affectionate amazement, as if it were silly but forgiveable to call the telephone wire a *shtrich.* I loved their apartment, all their books, pictures, knickknacks, and the smell of cigarette smoke. The first time I tasted non-kosher food was in their kitchen. My parents pulled Lynn off the balcony. They took her in and cared for her. Eventually she called her sister in Texas and her sister came up to New York for her. Not long afterward she died in an old-age home in Texas.

When she walks she carries herself as if she were a bowl of water which must not be allowed to spill. If you notice her posture, the stillness at the center, you might call it poise, but it's not poise, it's more like the tension you see in tightrope walkers.

He phones, reminds me that I said we could have dinner this coming week, as if I were morally committed to having dinner with him. I have become his obsession. As he talks he clears his throat and talks slowly, methodically, enunciating every syllable without pity for the little sounds. In the evenness of his enunciation there is something brutal. He defines my obligation—I said we could have dinner. He asserts it, clears his throat, and talks slowly and evenly, and then seems almost to beg. Why does he need my friendship? His wife is less than half his age. He got what he wanted, but doesn't sound happy. He discovered, maybe, that he didn't want what he got.

After a while, if you live long enough, you begin to meet the same people again and again. They have changed their names, of course, and they look more or less different, but there is no mistaking a person you have met before. It makes me think there is no self. If there is no self, there is no responsibility. Anyone can do anything to anybody.

June 22, '89

Last night up late talking to Katya on the telephone, a feeling of how our communion deepens. Earlier today, hurrying, I gave her a passing hello, and then I began thinking what the hell is the matter with me, I should have stopped. I remembered her look. She expected more. I'm too accessible to too many people, but she's special. I phoned her. On the phone, she talked about Priscilla, about whom she knows nothing, but imagines she's similar to Priscilla in regard to not judging people, and seeing that all people make equal claims on our love and concern. In fact, they both judge others plenty. There is no other similarity. Katya is exceedingly precise. Priscilla could be maddeningly vague except when contradicting me. Then she became clear, precise, and looked much taller.

Priscilla's mother once made a tie for me out of a beautiful silk print. She was a first-class seamstress, but the silk bunched up slightly just below the knot. I would pull the material down to smooth the tie, but the bunching up soon returned. There had been a tiny mistake in the construction. I changed the position of the knot, but the bunching always reappeared in another place. I took it as a criticism of me, and finally put the tie out of sight in the back of a closest.

Katya says she's afraid that if she thinks about what bad thing might happen she will have to live it. I have similar fears. It's also possible to think good things that might happen. I've lived my good thoughts and been disappointed by the difference between them and actual experience. You live or you think. It's well known that for the dramatic thrill some people imagine living amid terrible dangers, where the worst things might happen—as in mountain climbing—and the worst things do happen, worse than they could have imagined. It's like the Grimm's fairy tale where the children want to go outside in the night, though they are warned about the nightmare. They go anyway and the nightmare gets them.

March 3, '91
The Couple: She had a dream in which her boyfriend was sleeping with her sister. The dream was so real that it woke her up. She got dressed and drove to her boyfriend's house. He was sleeping with her sister. As she looked through the window she admitted to herself that she wanted her boyfriend to sleep with her sister. She loved both of them and wanted her sister to have everything she had. She had even told her sister to stay at her boyfriend's house until she found her own place. She was aware of her responsibility for what had happened. Still, seeing her boyfriend in bed with her sister made her wild. Using a garden hose, she filled a pail with water and carried it into the house and dumped it on them. Her sister dressed and ran out of the house and spent the rest of the night in a motel. None of them has ever mentioned the incident.

Gombrowicz contrasts nudists cavorting on a beach with "a dog trotting by in its canine elegance." His contrast makes good sense, but a dog has nothing on people who go naked in the jungles of Brazil or New Guinea or elsewhere.

March 20, '91
The Couple: She continues to see her former boyfriend. Her lover should be jealous, but when she tells him about the evenings with her ex she goes into so much detail that he imagines—or unconsciously assumes—she has told him everything, and there is no reason to feel jealous. If she didn't go into so much detail, he'd wonder what she isn't telling him. She isn't lying, and yet every word is a lie. She doesn't say, "Nothing happened," and he doesn't ask.

The Couple: She told me that her former boyfriend hadn't been with a woman for months. Then he met a woman through an ad in the personals. She was gorgeous. I wondered why she wasn't jealous, then realized that she'd be insulted if her former boyfriend took up with a woman less good-looking than herself. He felt lucky and happy, she said. The woman had suffered a painful divorce. Her husband stole all their property and abandoned her and their child, a little girl. The woman lives in a tiny apartment and works as an editor for a trade magazine. It pays for rent and food, but little more. She lives in terror of her ex-husband, thinking he will take away her little girl. The woman told all this on their first date. After that she talked only about their relationship. They've had three dates and she has talked of nothing else. He says if she keeps on talking about their relationship he will leave her.

July 7, '91

During dinner at David and Jane's, I argued with Toni, as if I had to take a stand on the issue of a union for graduate student instructors, which is important to her but of only indirect interest to me. I think professors, from highest to lowest rank, ought to teach their own classes as in the old days. Later, as I walked her to her car, she said, "I'm sorry there was such disagreement at dinner." I said, "It was all right. It made me understand my feelings. Visceral stuff. Unanalyzed." Why couldn't I say I was sorry, too, since that's what I felt?

July 9, '91

I behave badly and then can't write because my handwriting looks immoral. I feel morally poisoned. I can't write about that. I can't write anything. Not even a letter. If I'd been born in England or France or somewhere in Europe, I'd have been trained as a child to write in consistently good style. It wouldn't be inadvertently expressive of my moral condition. Europeans have consistently good or acceptable handwriting. The main difference between Europeans and Americans is that we can't help giving ourselves away. I am reminded of what Stent said when I asked him to write an essay for *The State of the Language*. He said he would like to contrast English speakers with speakers of other European languages. The other languages are loaded with formulas. English isn't. One must be constantly inventive when speaking English. Therefore, you can judge the quality of an English speaker. But French or German speakers are rather hard to judge. The formulas hide the speakers, make them sound better than they are. I said that's a good idea for an essay. He said he had no time to write it.

Months pass before I'm clean again and my handwriting looks O.K. At last I can write something that looks acceptable. When I behave badly, I tell myself that I'm not different from other people, and most behave much worse, and an enormous number would behave as badly as I do if they could, but they lack imagination or courage or occasions for being bad. No matter what I think, being bad uglies my handwriting. I can't bear to look at it. When I told all this to Peter he told me that he'd bought a horse. He said he keeps his horse stabled nearby. He said he loves his horse, and that she is superior to all the other horses in the stable. He said she is actually offended by the other horses because she is so sensitive. I supposed he was telling me about his instinctive life, as represented by his horse. As if I had no idea of what he might be telling me, I plunged back into the subject of being bad, or debauch, this time talking about the girl in Alabama. Peter said, "Who would pass up the experience?" He meant the girl, not me. I'd never supposed she did what she did only not to pass up the experience. It had nothing to do with love. I don't believe that's true, but that's how Peter and I talk to each other without talking to each other. I was personal and direct. Peter responded with feeling, but no matter how much he loves his horse, it's a horse. I persist in talking my way. He persists in his. We never destroy the civilized distinction, or tension, between personal and impersonal. Of course I try to do that, but he won't permit it.

Nov. 25, '91

Called Tom. He sounded nervous. He said Klaus Kinski died, apparently of natural causes; he was sixty-four, trying to write a book while living alone in Lagunitas, in a semi-wild, isolated area. He'd been at Tom's party for Norman Mailer, along with Melissa Gold and Bill Graham, who were killed in a helicopter crash. Three people who were at that party are dead. None were close to me, and I'd never have met them except through Tom. Melissa had an appealing face, natural warmth, and was easy to like. Graham was distant and had a tough demeanor, but was much loved. A Russian Jew, the dark face and physical type somewhat like mine. He and I had worked in Catskill hotels, years ago, where we first heard Latin music. Jews were crazy about it. Maybe they heard some ancient racial strain in the melodies and measure. Graham said, one night at Grossinger's, Machito's sister asked him to dance with her, and she said he was good. He felt honored. He said he preferred Latin music to rock, but wouldn't produce Latin music concerts for fear of offending "Latin heavies." It was their music, their culture, he said.

One night at Kimbal's East, I sat with Graham watching the dancers mambo. They looked good to me, but Graham said, "They're dancing on one, not two. They're betraying their culture." He meant the dancers were surrendering to a waltz-feeling, not the snap and hesitation of the syncopated African beat. I'd heard the same remark from Daniel, an Israeli, one night at Cesar's. After watching the dancers, he said, "They do it wrong." He got up and approached two beautiful Mexican women who were dancing together. Excellent dancers, I thought. He didn't. He asked them to dance with him and insisted they do it right. "Listen to the conga drum, not the bass," he said, and then he danced with both women at once, all moving to the African syncopation.

A very good dancer was a black woman who worked as a nurse in Oakland. She said her pleasure came when she felt the music in the man, the way it lived in his body. She was much in demand, never could sit long enough to finish her drink. Another woman, a very pretty blonde who always came alone to The Dock, always left alone—no girlfriends, no boyfriends. She loved to dance and received many invitations, but turned down most. I asked her why. She said, "The numbers are long. You don't want to be dancing with the wrong guy." She meant the same more or less as the nurse—about feeling the music in the man—but she wasn't as receptive or accepting. She wanted a man consistent with the music in herself. For the same reason, maybe, she had no boyfriend, though she was very pretty. Maybe she had a boyfriend who didn't dance, but I doubt that he'd have let her come here alone. There was no boyfriend. Between men and women, dancing is as subtle as anything else.

I heard that Carol Clover says, "Sex is for people who can't dance." Couples who looked great to me sometimes left the floor dissatisfied with each other. As they left the floor, I once heard a man say to his partner, "You want some advice? Take small steps." Dancing, like marriage, can look good from the outside, and be displeasing inside. The opposite is also true. A divorced couple at Cesar's danced beautifully together, then separated when the number ended and went to their respective tables. They smiled while dancing, but never talked during or afterward because they detested each other. Even so they couldn't resist dancing together. Then they became a single body through which the music flowed beautifully, as if they were in love.

With Kinski, whom I met twice, there was no conversation. He talked nonstop and had extraordinary energy, but he talked beyond me to the world, or an imaginary crowd standing behind me in the room. Even when he fixed my eyes with his stare, he seemed to talk straight through my head. I asked if he saw his daughter often. He said, "Not since the last time I fucked her." Such sudden and astonishing fury. I didn't know what he intended. Apparently, they didn't get along. Everything with him was ferociously personal.

Phone call. No answer when I say hello, but the line remains open, someone listening to me say hello, hello, hello.

Dec. 5, '91

I ran into a woman who remembered meeting me twenty-two years ago. She reminded me that I'd rented her house on Josephine Street. Jesse was born when we lived in that house. The woman appeared at my side and started talking to me as I stood at a counter in Andronico's looking at marinated olives. Her enthusiasm was surprising. There was warmth and pleasure in her expression, and she never stopped smiling as she reminded me of who she was. She didn't remember that she'd refused to return my cleaning deposit when the lease was up, claiming that her house hadn't been well cleaned.

Priscilla and her mother, both exceptionally careful and thorough workers, had spent a whole day cleaning the house, washing windows that seemed never to have been washed before, and scouring ancient tarlike grime off the linoleum floor of the kitchen.

The woman's face came back to me as she talked. In twenty-two years it hadn't changed for the worse. She looked quite good.

Apparently, her conscience was good. She had no sense of the con-
tradiction between her present warmth and her behavior in the
past when she tried to keep my deposit money. Because the woman
was Jewish, her petty avariciousness in front of my gentile wife and
mother-in-law embarrassed me. They were willing to let the cleaning deposit go—only a hundred dollars—but not me. I started to
clean the house again with fanatical determination. Without a word
they joined me and we redid the job already done, cleaning what
had been deeply cleaned. I scrubbed, scoured, mopped, and dragged
the vacuum cleaner from room to room. When the woman came
back the next day she glanced around casually, then handed over the
hundred-dollar deposit, but not because she saw that the house had
been cleaned well. She'd seen that the first time.

Meeting the former landlady reminded me that Allen and Deirdre
visited the house on Josephine Street and stayed for a few days. They
took care of Ethan while I went to the hospital to see Priscilla and
our new baby. Allen was driving a sports car, a Triumph. He tended
to drive the way he walked, weaving somewhat. About then, a man
phoned and said he was John Updike. He'd be in San Francisco the
following day and would like to meet me. He had a stammer. I offered to pick him up at the airport and drive him to the East Bay,
but he said he'd take "the shuttle." There was no shuttle. Nobody
here used that word. I figured he was from the east coast, maybe
Boston, and he really was John Updike. He never called again.
There was another strange phone call from a man who asked me to
accept the long-distance charges. The operator didn't give me his
name but said he calls himself a friend of Henry Miller. I accepted
the charges. The man then told me that he knew we'd get along.
Could I lend him money? Another time, late at night, Jerzy Kosinski phoned. He really was Kosinski. There'd been a bad review of

his new novel in the *Times*. The review was written by Bob Alter, my colleague. Kosinski was very upset and wanted me to account for Alter's review. Me?

I remembered driving with Allen from Davis to Berkeley. He was reading a story I'd just finished. As he read, the wind caught one of the pages, tore it out of his hand and out the car window. Allen said, "Pull over. I'll run back and get it." I told him Puccini wrote operas in bed and when a page slipped and fell onto the floor, he'd write a whole new page. I could do that, too.

May 23, '92

Sunday afternoon. Walking in northside Berkeley. A sign: "Estate sale." People going in and out of a house. Somebody died. About to pass the house when I see Raquel and Bud. They're going into the house. I join them. A hospital bed is in the middle of the living room. I look away. Somebody died right here. I walk to another room. Junk mail piled on a table. An envelope is addressed to Vlastos. I'm startled. I'm in his house. I wasn't invited. It suddenly feels like an angry house. I start to flee, then think I'll say goodbye to Raquel and Bud first. I look for them. They aren't anywhere. Notice a bookcase. A few books scattered on the shelves. Maybe the others were sold. I should leave. Should say goodbye, but I pick up a book, an Everyman's Library edition. Yellow cover. Descartes, *A Discourse on Method*. I flip through pages looking for marginalia. Sure enough, comments in small scribbled script, lightly penciled. The book now feels precious. Seventy-five cents. I buy it. Raquel and Bud are outside, lingering on the sidewalk, waiting to say goodbye. I show the book and say it belonged to the great Vlastos. I babble. Did you know this was his house? They're unimpressed. I feel awkward, futile, beside the point. Enough. Goodbye. At home I go through the pages searching for marginalia. Two little words stop me. Where Descartes says, "I had . . . a most earnest desire to know how to distinguish the true from the false, in order . . . to discriminate the right path in life," Vlastos underlined the sentence and scribbled, "Not serious!"

June 12, '92

Candace phoned. I recognized her voice. She sounded exhausted and hoarse, as if she'd been up all night. She said, "I saw you at the lecture yesterday. You were there, weren't you?"

"Yes."

"I know. I saw you."

"So?"

"Why did you ignore me?"

"I didn't see you."

"It wouldn't have been hard to say hello. I need some kind of social acknowledgment from you."

"I didn't say hello because I didn't see you."

"You looked right at me. You were with a woman. That's why you didn't say hello to me. Admit it."

"I didn't see you."

"Are you ever alone? Do you ever think that you might die alone?"

"Everyone dies alone."

"Being alone is easy if you have somebody. It's not if you have nobody."

"What do you say we meet for lunch."

"Why?"

"I want to see what you look like."

"You know what I look like."

"I mean it's been a very long time. You said that yourself."

"I never said that. Now you've had your obligatory little chat with me. Thanks. Goodbye."

I told Michael about the phone call, and said I was upset. He said, "That's the advantage of being married. You don't care what the wife says." I told Nym about the phone call and she said, "A woman who hasn't achieved much in life needs a lot of male attention. The requirements of an affair are more severe than a marriage. Are you having an affair with this woman?" I'm not married to Candace, we're not having an affair, and I have no idea if she hasn't achieved much. People talk from within, blind to another person's view. Maybe nobody ever talks to anybody. It gets more difficult all the time with computers, answering machines, and noisy restaurants. No wonder TV "talk" shows are popular. A silent population gapes at people talking, as if it were a miracle.

July 1, '92
She says, "I want to go someplace away from everyone."
I say, "Why?"
She says, "So I can be really beautiful."

July 5, '92
Long walk in woods behind Larkspur with Mary. She told me a dream. An old woman pursued her, wanted to bite her. The next night Mary prepared to confront the old woman by going into a semi-trance before falling asleep. The old woman appeared. Mary said, "Why do you do this to me?" The old woman said, "Why do you do it to me?" I thought it was a touching and hilarious dream, and asked Mary's permission to write it, maybe publish it. She said I could, but I mustn't name her. How strange. Compared to other stuff she's told me, none of which I'd repeat, the little dream is utterly innocuous.

July 7, '92

Went to dinner with Louisa at Teddy and Elaine's. They're renting a house in Tiburon. Two or three thousand a month, but the insurance company is paying. They lost everything in the Oakland fire. The house is for sale. Over a million bucks. I thought, "I'll never own a house like this." We toured the rooms. Fantastic view of the bridges and the bay. Could I live in that house? I couldn't. I'd feel there is nothing left to want. Sooner live in a monk's cell. Driving home after dinner, it's very dark. Can't see trees or water. I'm hypnotized by the road, the meal, the wine, the headlights. Louisa snoozing, slumped against the door. I start talking, as if only to myself. I forgot she's twelve years old. She said, "Stop." I said, "Why?" She said, "I don't want to hear it." I said, "If I can't talk to you, who can I talk to?" She said, "Just stop it." I said, "Why?" She said, "Dad, I'm like a little flower, and you're watering me—by pissing on me." She giggled, amused by the idea of herself trying to be a kid.

Aug. 5, '92

If Becky looked the least bit different we might never have met. For example, if her hair were faintly red she might be in Buenos Aires or Budapest or New Orleans this minute, carried away by an architect or pilot or lawyer or politician or moron. She said she likes morons. "Mmmmm," she says, "a moron." Very painful, but I must get used to the idea. Nothing beats a moron.

Jan. 9, '93

To understand another person in her feelings is possible only without analysis. When she is angry, and I try to be rational, it makes her angrier. I can't even make myself seem calm, since that too is an affront to her condition, as if I were telling her, in my calm demeanor, not to feel what she feels. Feelings fight to the death. In regard to myself, I can be completely rational. I even made a list of characteristics that describe me—an objective list—and I gave it to the doctor. I said, "It will save us time."

"But this list is your problem," he said.

Jan. 10, '93
I'd never write about being happy. It's of no interest as a dramatic subject. Being sad feels personal, even unique.

Cats are the only animals, aside from humans, who kill for pleasure. Unlike dogs, they never lose themselves in a happy emotion. Self-possession, a cool sense of personal boundaries.

Jan. 11, '93
Peter says that insight, or understanding, rises all at once from the unconscious. It isn't gradually gathered, rationally accumulated, or logically derived. If it were, it would feel wrong. There are people who know you instinctively, and they are right. Others "figure you out," and get nothing right. In the history of philosophy, systematic thinkers have dismissed their predecessors for thinking incorrectly. In over two thousand years none have ever gotten anything right. For example, I never heard anyone say, "Spinoza was right."

Jan. 23, '93
One feeling becomes another, like notes in a melody—the melody of life—beginning here, ending there, la, la, la.

Burt Welcher said, "The first time you prefer to stay home and work, or do anything instead of going to see her, break up." You imagine love will be discovered with another person, but you expect too much. Nothing less than too much. "Question not the need," says King Lear. This is the basis of capitalism. Nobody ever said, "I have enough money." Georg Simmel contrasts money with love, saying the desire for permanent union in love often turns into disaffection and revulsion when the object is attained, but this isn't the case with money. The need for more is endless. If people questioned the need, and stopped yearning for more, the economy would collapse. Affairs are brief unless there is a lot of sex, but the need for love of another human being is endless. If it were a need for God, we'd never invest in persons.

Raphael's portrait of La Muta seems more real than the woman who sat for it, rather as though the portrait had always existed independently. La Muta, in her silence, speaks of a reality elsewhere. The mystery of a face is the mystery of all images.

Awake again at three A.M., angry, thinking I've been good to people who repaid me with pain. But God did good and wasn't repaid in kind. He said we are "evil in our imagination." So who am I to feel sorry for myself? When I complained to Barney Simon about betrayal, he smiled and said, "My back is a tissue of scars."

Feb. 3, '93
In my novel everything about the woman is interesting to the hero—how she does her makeup, how she dresses, how she puts on her clothes. He listens to her voice for meanings unknown even to herself. He watches the movement of her eyes to see what she sees and thinks . . . His kind of absorption is a curse. He knows her too well, too much, never enough. He is addicted to knowing her. His attention is a pain in the ass. He will lose her.

Feb. 10, '93
A cat weighs as much as a baby, and you can carry it around as you would a baby. A cat sleeps as much a baby. Cats and babies are very old.

My writing feels warm until I revise, make it better, and then it gets cold. I should revise further, mess up my sentences, make them warm, make money.

It was and it wasn't a nice apartment. High ceilings, good light, but the air had a greasy feel and carried a sweetness like rotting fruit, maybe a melon in the kitchen garbage can. The walls needed fresh paint. There were cracks in the plaster that hadn't been mended. An old Persian rug, with an insanely complicated design, sent weird vibrations up through my shoes. I thought of sharp-eyed kids tying the knots, going blind.

Oct. 17, '93

At the end of the evening, I was about to make the long drive home when a horde of Josie's friends arrived, excited people with shining eyes and extravagant gestures. A feverish gaiety. They were actors, part of Josie's new social life in the movie business. They made witty remarks in all directions, laughing at everything. Exaggerated laughter, a bit forced, almost as if they might otherwise collapse with grief. It was late, but they needed a stage and audience. Actors give the most of any artists, and are the most deformed by their profession.

Brodsky said a poem should be delivered every day with the groceries. I've never had groceries delivered, but can imagine the kid screaming, his diaper loaded, and I have to clean him up, feed him, hurry to work. What's this? A poem in the groceries? Like Robinson Crusoe finding the footprint, maybe.

Oct. 18, '93

The least necessary are most admired. They play at flying a plane, performing surgery, practicing law, being a parent, etc. They act, imitating necessary things people do. In *Mephisto,* H. Mann opposes theater to fascism. Compared to fascism, everything human is playacting. Between the former and the latter there is a never-ending war.

Ritualized drama, as in ancient Greece or China, is anti-natural, but so minutely controlled as to seem full of necessity; inevitable. Anti-natural and like nature.

I said there is evidence that the boy murdered the girl. Erika said, "No, he is my friend. Anyhow, which would you rather believe?" Christopher Lasch calls this narcissism. What people prefer to believe, etc. But why is it important to her what I believe, or anyone believes?

Moods are so oppressive they make the simplest action difficult. Possessed by a mood, I say things I'd never say otherwise. I become drunk on feeling. What emerges isn't me. It's as if I were possessed by an adjective—cold, hilarious, obnoxious, depressed. "The greenhouse never so badly needed paint," writes Wallace Stevens, contemplating his death. He thinks he has run out of adjectives. "The greenhouse" is the world, and "paint" is the adjective that is badly needed by the world. The world has lost its color—its green, its adjective, its romance, flavor, smack, hope, imaginative substance. He says what remains is "The Rock," or the universal gravestone. As death approaches, Stevens sees the rock, or "the thing," what he calls "the the."

Henry Roth told me that when he was an ignorant kid, he tried to understand T. S. Eliot's tone. "The meaning of the poetry wasn't clearly offered," said Henry, "so it wasn't worth worrying about." We were in his study. It was late and he was very tired. He didn't want me to leave. He wanted to say something. His face shone with perspiration, his voice was slow and gravelly, his words were slurred. He was almost ninety years old and sick. I heard every word, but not the thing he wanted to say, only that he wanted to say it. Maybe I heard more than I know. If I kept on describing the moment it might emerge. He seemed small and crumpled in the large chair he used for writing. His skin looked yellowish and hot. If he let go, he'd fall asleep instantly. He said, "I've lived too long," as if he were lingering in someone's house at the end of a party. He felt he should leave, go home, and let others go to sleep, but things remained to be said. His idea of trying to understand Eliot's tone seemed spiritually superb in a kid from the Bronx. Didn't occur to him to be awed by Eliot's unintelligibility. A comparison of Roth and Bellow might be interesting. Great poets, but Bellow was successful. Roth, ferociously resentful of Bellow's success in a decaying society, was strangled by righteous politics and moral self-disgust.

Phone calls, lunches, coffees, dinner parties, endless social motion— desperate nourishment, but a way of being—Being-in-relationship. Alone, one starves. Being-in-relationship is family. The primal "I need you," what lovers once said.

In blood, bloodiness.

They come toward you, anxious to be with you, or anyone but themselves, so they make themselves seductive, offer endless attention, flattery, love, sexual cornucopias. If you desire them as they desire you, they flee.

I'm talking and laughing when I notice Josie staring at me. In the expression of her eyes she seems hurt, as if she's been denied something. I think she imagines I'm enjoying a pleasure unavailable to her, but I'd let her take my place, sit with these people and do the talking and laughing. I'd be grateful if she would. I want nothing she can't have.

Over the years Morgan has been shrinking, shriveling, collapsing inward like a sun-dried fruit. His body bends over itself, as if he were perpetually reading one of his innumerable books. His skin has grown tighter and harder against the bones. He reads and reads, searching for what he himself couldn't tell you—a sentence or a word, perhaps, that will make it possible to stop reading. But of course he will never stop until he goes blind or drops dead. You'd suppose he was a Jew, an ancient man of the book, but he is the product of Catholic schools, and his mind isn't much like a Jew's. It's Jesuitical rather, exceedingly fine, exceedingly sharp, with nothing sensual or humorous in the energy of its discriminations. In conversation, he can be as moralistic and funny as a Jew, but he somehow remains dispassionate, detached, dry, hard. He lives in infinite space, like a distant star. In the old days, I'd ache for his company and rush to meet him. We'd sit in his room listening to the unaccompanied cello suites on his phonograph, and drink bourbon. I loved the bleakness of his room—whites, grays, blacks—the same colors in the music. I remember the look of the yellow bourbon, the delicious singular heat. Then he got married. I got married. Nothing could be the same. These days I must look up his phone number every time I phone him. Women have been more influential in my life, but that's irrelevant. In regard to almost any of the women, there might well have been another woman. Only a few seemed my fate. As for Morgan, there was nobody else. He shows me pictures of his kids. What's the point of it? He loves his kids, and I love mine, but what have the pictures got to do with the thing between us?

———

She has distracting mannerisms, a way of bringing up childlike, playful, emotional irrelevancies. Never allows pure focus on a subject, but tilts things slightly, makes you see from her angle. She always "has an angle." The expression "an angle" reminds me of how little I can say that hasn't been said better. English speaks me, and it isn't even my native tongue.

Nov. 13, '93
He wanted to talk to S. She didn't want to talk to him. I got stuck, unable to talk to either of them, unable to leave. It was a small room. Crowded. I had nowhere to go and couldn't disengage where I wasn't engaged. I was miserable. M. wanted to fuck S., virtually doing it with his fixed gaze. S. kept looking away, unwilling to be fixed, let alone fucked. She tried to include me in the flight of her eyes. She needed company, needed rescue. M. wouldn't look at me. He leaned toward her and talked, determined to make her listen to him, see him, only him, though she wasn't fascinated, wasn't fuckable, but he'd committed himself, and was no less trapped than me. I felt sorry for him as he persisted, couldn't relent, persisted in trying to engage and seduce. She needed another drink and another cigarette between her face and his ardor.

F. speaks to us in measured phrases, very rational, enormously sane, obviously concerned to appear sane, but he is too controlled, too rational. He denies that he's an alcoholic. That isn't what we heard, but poor F. thinks he has a reputation as a drunk. It would be best if he didn't imagine what people say. Even if he guessed right, it can't be corrected. "Do nothing," I told him. "Say nothing. Nobody thinks you're an alcoholic. Besides, people forget after a while. They think mainly about themselves." But F. is obsessed. If anyone told him what people say, he'd kill himself.

Nov. 26, '93

Jayne doesn't want to come to dinner. She can't smoke here. It's nice of her to give a reason. We pretend to believe it's the real reason, and we remain friends. The real reason is that she thinks I treated her girlfriend badly. I didn't, but the fact is irrelevant. The important thing is to pretend she can't smoke here. Life goes on regardless of facts, and not otherwise.

A waitress led us to a table.

Beard said, "You're new."

"I'm from Minnesota. I arrived last week."

She glanced back, smiling teeth.

Beard said, "I'm crazy about Minnesota."

We took chairs.

"The weather is hard," she said, her smile unchanged.

"You can hunt bears," said Beard.

"You hunt bears?" The smile vanished, her upper lip twisting as if she smelled something bad.

"Me? You kidding? Of course not."

When she left, Beard said, "Bitch."

Dec. 10, '93

Hawaii. I saw a man with leg muscles so large it seemed their main job was to carry themselves. He was standing outside the restaurant talking to a woman, constantly adjusting his posture, stretching his leg muscles. He was short and dark, with close-cropped hair, a receding chin. His nose was slightly hooked. Broad shoulders, short arms, fingertips reaching no farther than his crotch. He'd have to bend forward to hold his cock while peeing.

This journal goes about with me like another person, collecting my thoughts and observations. They are important to nobody, not even me, but I'd have a fit if the journal were lost. People talk, giving themselves to the memories of others. Society is a memorial institution, but remembers only what it is able to hear, which isn't always what you say. It hears what it can understand, or wants to hear. I'm told I said things I couldn't have said, and didn't. As in the old days, reading a student's notes after my class, I'd think—helplessly— I didn't say that.

When it's news it's too late. Murder, rape, kidnap . . . Can't be undone. After a while the newspapers stop talking about it and it's not news. The Holocaust never ceases being news. Again and again Isaac Rosenfeld's remark comes to mind. The Nazis proved murder is "feasible." It's all the news there is.

Gray day. Small rain. Then brightness in the late afternoon. No dramatic cloud shows. At night the stars are numerous and brilliant. It's windy. Only a few mosquitoes. Dinner was seafood bisque, salad, apple crisp. I am reading the biography of Richard Burton. He arrives in India in 1842, goes to Baroda, acquires a native wife, probably a Muslim courtesan. He could speak over twenty languages, but wasn't a social type, always going off to exotic and dangerous parts of the world. A military spy, he sometimes wore a disguise. He belonged nowhere. He could be anywhere. Brilliant, supremely courageous, indestructible, but not exactly good. He couldn't be good. Good means staying at home, in your village, your house, your room, and behaving like everyone else. Readers stay in one place. To read a novel you must sit still. Novels—no matter what they are about—are about being good.

The old men sit with slumped postures, and very still for hours. They seem to be thinking, "What did I do wrong to have arrived here in this condition?"

Dec. 12, '93

Birdcalls wake me, a sound like names, like the trees repeating themselves in the dawn mist, each holding its place, awaiting recognition, like names.

Lava streaming into the ocean with plumes of toxic gas. I walked the black crust of the lava field. Oily, slick-looking, glittery surface. Then ropelike, black, concentric coils, and then bulbous protuberances. The lava crust crunches glassily underfoot. Hot sun, blue sky, steam, and these vast black fields of glittery petrified turbulence.

Dec. 14, '93

Drive to Akaka Falls in the rain. Fans of gigantic bamboo, and deep cool shadowy gulches, and roaring water. Then on to Honakaa and browsing in the vintage-clothing and antique shops, then to Pahoa and dinner. Love intensifies the most banal experience, everything gains wonder. But she starts crying. She says, "I'm homesick." I go and sit on a bench. She follows and pleads, "Forgive me." I'm the one who needs forgiveness, having dragged her to this place where nothing for her is fantastically beautiful or exciting. She wants only to go home.

Dec. 18, '93

Puna coast, Kalani Honua, near Pahoa. Three gay men are in the next room. One is sick, coughing all night. I hear birdcalls, strong wind, the sea advancing in the distance, rain slapping leaves and roof and then it becomes a heavy insistent rain and it blots out other sounds but the coughing. The rain grows still more intense. I'm apprehensive. There must be a consummation to such force, but none comes. There is only loud continuous rain. It beats on the wide green shining leaves of the coconut palms and banana palms and mango trees and the masses of ohia leaves, splattering and sliding down into the vegetable earth and porous lava, into deeper and deeper layers of lava. It's loud and scary, this rage against nothing.

Waves hit the black lava coast of Puna and shoot thirty feet up into the air in a white shape, a wall which then flares and becomes a huge white booming tree—almost a word.

Brain rubs world. Thoughts are friction.

No word for weather in Hawaiian, for music in Swahili, for God in Hebrew.

People here work, love, die, fight, kill, steal, connive, take drugs, commit suicide, build houses. Against people nature stands in magnificent indifference.

In comedy, spirit triumphs over matter. In tragedy, matter over spirit.

Dec. 19, '93

I remembered again my lunch with Beard, how the waitress returned with two glasses of wine, hurried, a bit flustered, and Beard asked for a pasta. I asked for soup and salad. We had to raise our voices against the noise. "Have more," said Beard, shouting. "My treat."

"This is all I have for lunch."

"Make an exception. Try the swordfish."

"I don't know . . ."

"You don't like swordfish?" He gaped, amazement enlarging his eyes and mouth, his face becoming one hole of incredulity. "Not like swordfish?"

"I'll have it."

"Bring my friend the swordfish," he said; loud, arrogant.

"Do you still want soup and salad?" said the waitress, smiling mechanically, disguising her impatience.

"Of course he does. Bring, bring."

I felt an urge to kill myself.

The antique shop owner in Hawaii, a blustery old man, sold me his one authentic piece, a carved pig. He wanted to get rid of it. Everything else was new shiny stuff—carved elephants, gods, puppets. The pig was old, roughly carved, not shiny. It was the only thing in a shop full of brand-new junk that had value. It was the only thing for which you couldn't substitute another commodity—shoes, hats, jewelry, a can of tuna fish. Its value was in itself, its lines and proportions, and had no relation to the price people will pay. The carved pig wasn't great art. Still, it belonged in the same realm as a painting by Titian, or any work of art that gives value to money. It's never the other way around. Value lies in the relation of fact and symbol, says Friedlander. Value is always in the relation, and beyond analysis. Unless you see value you have nothing to say about literature, painting, music, etc. The old man said, "Eighty dollars." His wife, a Hawaiian, was sitting with a crouched posture on a stool in a corner, bent as if expecting a blow. She muttered, "The man from L.A. offered four hundred dollars." The owner bellowed, "The man from L.A. isn't here, is he?" He'd been embarrassed, and he was furious at his wife for speaking up. I gave him eighty dollars. I'd have paid more. In his fury at his cowering muttering wife, the owner took bitter pleasure. He'd asked eighty dollars, as if to strike a blow at her and the man from L.A. He sold the pig to spite them, a blow against himself, too. He knew the pig was good. The body is long, the head is long. Fijian cannibals called people "long pigs," says Ronald Wright in *On Fiji Islands*.

Dec. 20, '93

Beard had written a poem and wanted to read it to me on the telephone. It was the middle of the day. He starts reading. The poem was endless. I thought I'd go crazy. I told him I heard the doorbell and had to go answer. I'd phone him back in a minute. That was almost a year ago. Too late to apologize. He buys me lunch, as if he had been rude to me. I think of apologizing, but can't.

Some guy calls me. He would like to talk to me in person but understands that I don't have time for lunch with strangers. He's aggressively apologetic, almost rude. He insists that he doesn't want to impose, or hold me on the phone. I must tell him if I want to hang up. Just say it. I said I'd have lunch with him tomorrow. He said it was a lot to ask. He really appreciated it. I said the Faculty Club at noon, at the desk. We said goodbye and that's how it registered in my mind—goodbye, goodbye—and I never went to meet him.

Xmas '94

Walk along Bodega Head. Sea colors and thud of surf. Black jagged rocks. Cliffs of shattered shale. Yellow, green, red flowers sprouting in the crannies. Ooze of vegetal light. Blue, too. All primaries ooze. Incessant salt wind sears my cheeks and eyes. It shakes the cabin. Gulls slide at angles against the wind; surfing.

I noticed uncertain, almost spasmodic motions in my hands when I poured wine. In me looms doubt. Then I remembered the guy at Fran's, her former boyfriend. Still lean and youthful-looking, but life lay crushed in the softness of his voice. Defeated, slow, sleepy manner. He seemed pathologically relaxed, sprawling in the armchair, rather than comfortable, almost drugged-looking. Fran said he'd inherited a fortune, lived high, and then lost every cent through bad investments. So this is what it's like when you fall from money. The ghost of his former manner remained. Moved so slowly, as if trying to remember what it was like to move. Fran said he and I were born the same year. I'm nothing like that man.

July 21, '94
In traveling there is true solitude because for a while I am no place, and I spend money as if it had become less real.

You don't know what you're seeing when seeing it for the first time, but you see it as you never will again. Later, you wish you could escape sophistication and see innocently. This is what Heraclitus means when he says you can't step into the same river twice. Picasso said that when he was eight he could draw like Titian or Raphael, but he spent the rest of his life trying to draw like a child.

Aug. 31, '94
I imagine us meeting years later. We're old. We became old without each other. We'd have become old anyway. Without each other, at least we had real lives.

The *L. A. Times* asks me to do a book review and sends bound galleys. I read, make notes, start writing. Days pass. I do nothing but write the review. Then it occurs to me, I was asked for an opinion—praise, dispraise, contempt, adulation—a review, not a revelation.

Renoir said when he was a kid he upset a nun in his Catholic school with clever questions about her beliefs. A priest told him to cut it out and said there are things people cannot afford not to believe. Renoir laughed. I laughed, too, though it wasn't funny. The Book of Jonah ends on a similar note, but suggests there is much that we aren't equipped to understand.

Dec. 13, '94

The prophets heard the voice of God. They weren't called by pictures. Hearing is the most spiritual sense, but sight is first—"Let there be sight." It's also the hungriest, most vulgar, and most insatiable. You can shut your eyes and not see. You can't shut your ears. The visible world is easy to dismiss, but not the internal world of sound.

Dec. 14, '94

Marsha invites me to a party. I say, "O.K." Then she says sadly, "The people won't be interesting." We start laughing. She says, "Well, we can talk to each other." Could do that without the party, but now I really want to go. What are uninteresting people? Everybody is interesting to themselves, I think. Then I remember the months of insomnia, how Sonny would say, "The chatter in my head never stops." The moment she shut her eyes, she said, "I begin boring myself." She made me listen while she read aloud from a newspaper article on insomnia. A long article. It was about three A.M. The bed lamp was burning in my eyes. She kept nudging me. "Are you listening?"

Dec. 23, '94

Marsha's party. As promised, there were uninteresting people. Familiar types. Jog-bike-hot-tub-massage-eat-meditate-fuck-fly-around-the-world-California-people. Big house and not a book anywhere. Some guys in a corner played video games. I got a beer and joined them intending to kibitz, but there was no conversation. They made little grunts when the video motorcycle went off the road or smashed into something. I made grunts, too, but didn't feel accepted by the group. Couldn't grunt right. After about twenty minutes, I asked if I could try the game. The guy at the controls gave them to me and left the room. The others followed him. I pretended to be absorbed, like a jog-bike-hot-tub-kind-of-guy, though nobody watched me. Leaving the party, Becky said some guy told her he'd had a baby with his girlfriend, then said, "But that's all right." She repeated it with a question mark. "But that's all right?"

Feb. 28, '95

Watched an old movie. In one scene a man offers a cigarette to a woman who is in the midst of saying something. She stops and takes the cigarette. The interruption gives a touch of reality to the moment. It was invented by the actor to suggest the irrelevant and distracting business of life, or he offered the cigarette to show solidarity and help the actress relax and escape from herself. It occurred to me that you don't see movies. You watch them. At a painting you look. It doesn't move. Watching a movie, fixed in a seat, in the dark, motionless, you're completely rendered unto the action, and yet—motionless, hidden in darkness—watching feels predatory.

A man with an important face. His speech is rational, flat, full of careful hesitations as though he were fearful of belying the importance of his face. He exudes the pressure associated with caution. He worries about the expectations of other people. His every word is fragile; could be smashed by a look. He smokes cigarettes thoughtfully, feeling the dry cylinder pinched in his lips and fingers, feeling the heat in his lungs, and seems to reflect on these sensations. The least message from his lungs or viscera is of tremendous concern.

A woman lives next door. She does little except sing and entertain lovers. Her voice carries through her bedroom windows and the trees between our houses. I can hear her conversations with her lovers. "You contradict yourself," she often says. They tend to be handsome men who wear blue jeans, move slowly, and contradict themselves.

———

Coleridge says there is no such thing as a bad poem. There's no such thing as evil, only an absence of good. If it isn't good, the poem doesn't exist. F. R. Leavis called the novels of C. P. Snow "nullities."

March 6, '95
He gave her presents—shoes, coat, etc. She said, "He objectifies." Not allowing that he might be generous, she subjectifies.

Watched TV show on female models. The bodies seemed, however beautiful, invariably less than perfect. I was reminded of Kenneth Clark's remarks on the pathos of bodies, and the artist's transformation of the naked into the nude.

A corrosive spirit of disclosure is everywhere. It's complemented by the lust for confession, which is also everywhere, as evidenced in television shows, contemporary poetry, painting, and even this journal, a kind of talking as much as writing.

March 7, '95
"Once upon a time" introduces a kind of story, an old story that has been told much more than once, like fairy tales. It has a form, a promise of meaning. The kind of story beginning "It rained in Paris that day . . ." is modern. It's about mere life—place, weather, voices, a present moment. It promises sensation, nothing else.

In the gym go men with mountainous shoulders who never labored at anything but the look of themselves.

I took early retirement from the university and rarely had anything to do with departmental occasions.

April 3, '95

Asked to introduce Robert Stone when he gives his reading, I agree to do it. That night I have a dream. I'm on stage, making the introduction. Everybody is there. Fred Crews, Ralph Rader, Tom Flanagan. All my old colleagues. They're smart and critical. They expect me to make a fool of myself, so I'm scared. I have to be good. I begin by listing Stone's awards, and then carry on with a personal appreciation. I say Stone is in the tradition of American writers who deal with the subject of evil. Before Stone, I say, there was Flannery O'Connor. Before Flannery O'Connor, I say, there was Emily Dickinson. It seems like a wonderful insight, but suddenly Bob Hass stands up and very firmly says, "No!" He then recites a long poem by Emily Dickinson to prove she didn't write about evil. When he finishes I wake up. The clock on the night table says five A.M. I call Iowa City, where it's seven A.M. I have to speak to my little girl. I am upset, need to know she loves me. Bob answers in a sleepy voice. Domestic. Proper. Safe. I cry out, as if it were an astounding coincidence that he answered the phone, though it's his phone number—"Bob!" He says, "Yes." I'm grateful he's there, being a good stepfather, taking care of Louisa. All this happens in feelings, not thoughts, simply because Bob sounds sleepy. I begin raving, "I just had a dream and you were in it." He listens patiently. I recite the one line I remember of the poem: "The stair in the middle of the house." I tell him that once you go up "the stair in the middle of the house," you can't come down again until dawn, because there is something dangerous below. Then I ask if Emily Dickinson wrote such a poem. He says, "She should have, but I'm afraid she didn't."

Bob then gives Louisa the phone. I tell her what happened. She laughs. Later in the day, I phone to speak to her again. I say I know her mother thinks I'm crazy, but I'm worried about what Bob thinks. She says, "Oh, don't worry, Dad. He's thought you were crazy for a long time." She laughs. I explain that I've been taking a medication called colchicine. It has side effects, one being hallucinations. Louisa is laughing. The more I try to sound sane, the more she laughs. I go on, to keep her laughing. The sound does me good.

March 20, '95
I was the only one who had gone to the screening of the host's movie, and the only one not invited to his dinner. All of us had been invited to the screening, and we all expected the movie to be bad, but, since I was the only one who went to the screening, I was the only one guilty of actually knowing, as a matter of fact, that it was bad. Everyone but me was invited to dinner. I'd have had to lie and say the movie had redeeming elements—beautiful cinematography, clever plot, clever dialogue—though it had nothing. I couldn't say the movie was worse than bad, a huge waste of time and money. My own bad movie made me worry about losing friends.

Some European philosophers and modern jazz musicians practice unintelligibility, as if terrified of being understood, or as if clarity, verbal or musical, fails to represent their personal vision. "If you understand me, you don't understand me," says Lacan. But why bother being difficult? Not everyone can even learn to read. Among those who can, very few can read beyond literal sense. Why should anyone want to be hard to understand if hardly anyone understands much to begin with? Again the Book of Jonah, to which the orthodox turn on the highest of the holy days.

He is expected to be good, and it is possible for him to be very good. Instead, he is bad, and then thinks he is authentically himself, but this is only to say that he is not what others expect him to be.

Sartre rejected the Nobel Prize because he refused to accept the opinion of others about his value.

April 2, '95

Jesse's new girlfriend has bleached blond hair and dark eyebrows. The dark eyebrows set off by the bleached hair give her face a masklike disagreeable expression. Louisa says she heard the girl is "disagreeable." Apparently it's a contemporary style.

April 6, '95

When things work out for me it's good luck. When things go badly, it's the way it had to be—fate. "That it should come to this," says Hamlet.

April 7, '95

So many worries that it's hard to remember what matters.

Bad to discover at my age that my character needs correction.

David Lodge sends me bound galleys of *Therapy,* his new novel. It makes me happy. No jealousy, so I must truly love him. So happy that I immediately write him a letter, praising the novel. I haven't read more than three pages. I confess that I've read very little and say that the little is funny and engaging. Absolutely true. Say I'll finish it that night. Absolutely not true. I go on and on about other things, and the letter becomes long. I haven't seen David in years. I have a lot to say. I am getting a big kick out of listening to myself talk to him, making lots of jokes about my present bad luck. Lost the girl, computer crashed, very sick, attacked by reviewers, rejected by publishers and producers. I'm having a splendid time. I imagine him laughing. Then it occurs to me nobody writes letters anymore. Then I think: David will find my letter annoying. It will make him feel put upon, as though he has to respond in kind. Next he'll wonder if I'll keep his letter with my papers. Then he'll wonder if someday my kids will sell his letter through Sotheby's. I tear up my letter.

April 8, '95

Herb and Marion invite me to dinner at Chez Panisse. Herb asks what I'm reading. I say Bernard Williams, *Shame and Necessity,* and I babble about his discussion of Agamemnon sacrificing his daughter. Goes berserk. Hacks her up so the ships can sail off to war. Say it reminds me of the time I was fired by Buckwalter, headwaiter at the Nevele Country Club. Buckwalter, with his big belly and big black voice, accused me of stealing a steak, went berserk in the dining room, and fired me. Later, privately, he said my job was guaranteed for next summer, but I had to go now; I was the last waiter to be hired and the dining room was overstaffed. Just like what Aeschylus says about Agamemnon: Buckwalter "put on the harness of necessity" and went nuts, falsely accusing me, then firing me.

Marion then says, "Herb doesn't know how to fire anyone. He begins by praising, trying to protect the person's dignity. When he's finished the person has no idea he's been fired."

If I hadn't stayed up half the night reading about Agamemnon, I'd never have learned this about Herb, whom I've known since I was a kid. What did I learn? Herb Sandler, president of the third-largest savings and loan in America, has trouble firing people. I've always known he was a good guy.

April 15, '95

The trucks go all night along Interstate 80 with great speed and noise, as if possessed by an invincible determination to burst through the darkness not for a reason, not toward a goal, but for the sake of going, going, going.

April 16, '95
After watching the Simpson trial, I had no heart for a seder dinner, unable to forget the defense lawyers. They were reminiscent of the one described by Dostoyevski in his diary. He says his defense lawyer was determined to establish his innocence and writes: ". . . the thought that I, completely guilty, might suddenly walk out as completely innocent was so amusing, and also so appealing, that I must say this half-hour in court was among the most entertaining I have ever spent." Dostoyevski says a lawyer is "doomed to be dishonest, and this sad state of affairs is considered not an aberration but, on the contrary, a most normal order of things."

Alice Adams called. I said, "I'm not going to a seder." Why didn't I just say O.K.? She said, "Oh, that's all right. I'll ask you the questions." We made a date for dinner. Becky and I sat in Alice's living room, chatting before going out. She told us that, after her divorce, Paul Jacobs, a local writer (totally bald, I remember), fixed Alice up with Irving, who was teaching at Stanford. They'd never met. Minutes after Irving arrived at her apartment, he said, "You'd be a beautiful woman if it weren't for your teeth." After dinner, going home, Becky said, "You can see she was always a pretty woman and will always be. She's beautiful!" Becky was furious, still thinking about the story. I remembered seeing Jacobs at a party in the Berkeley hills during the sixties, and overhearing him talk to a local well-known cartoonist, somebody like Crumb but not as good. The cartoonist looked around and said, "This must be the home of an ecology pig." Jacobs ignored the comment and said, "I've long worshipped your drawings." In the exchange, I think I heard a cultural phenomenon.

April 25, '95

The wildest fantasy can be realized, but you mustn't then talk about it. Talk undoes experience retroactively. Listening to yourself, your story seems not so wild, and the other person's reaction can even make it seem deplorable. Then you feel pathetic for being excited by your adventure. Talking about it can arouse envy, anger, contempt, disgust, lingering ill will, and a desire to punish you severely. I should never have written the piece about Audrey in Hollywood. Michener said his wife hated it. Instantly I could feel my mistake, palpably, in my fingertips, the way Trotsky says he felt the emergence of a new social class.

May 2, '95

Robert Stone and five of us from the English department had dinner at the Faculty Club. I told him I had gout. He said, "I've had it for twenty-seven years." We talked about colchicine and the healing power of the crocus. He said the drug was discovered by an Egyptian physician in the twelfth century. There are mummies with gnarled bones indicating gout. I got excited by my relation to mummies, almost lost control, almost started raving about the features of gout—excess uric acid, purines, proteins, crystals in the joints—but remembered Stone had had gout much longer than I, and besides it was his evening.

May 8, '95. San Francisco

Norman Mailer was onstage at the Herbst theater, and afterward he went to the Tosca bar. He gave me my first colchicine, in 1987, in Havana, when my knee ballooned while dancing the mambo. Norman and his beautiful Norris, each taking an arm, helped me climb the steps of the Palacio, my knee raging and fat. Inside the marble hall Fidel was greeting visitors to the film festival. He wore his tailored green uniform and talked at length to Beatriz Valdez, the beautiful, talented actress who starred in *La Bella del Alhambra*. From the way he leaned toward her face and breasts, hands clasped behind his back, you could see Fidel approved of her politically. Someone said he has never danced the mambo, which is odd for a Latin male, but it's known that he loves to talk to women. A crowd arrived with Norman Mailer at the Tosca. The jukebox was blasting a soprano aria. Jeanette Etheredge asked what I thought of this party. I shouted, "There is no risk of conversation." She named people in the crowd. I listened carefully and forgot each name.

Eldridge Cleaver arrived with Cecil Brown. Eldridge said he'd found his landlord's sister sleeping in his bed, wearing his nightgown, and that she'd taken all his papers, which he'd spent months arranging, and thrown them on the floor in a big pile and then kicked them. He stopped talking to us when a beautiful blond girl walked by. He said, "Well, hello to you," then resumed talking about his landlord's sister. He said he intended to study her when she was "released."

I sat beside Norman, who was drinking boilermakers and signing copies of his new book. He said chasing beer with bourbon is superb for the smoothness. He was attentive to everyone who approached, a rare thing in the higher social flux. He looked better and better, signing, talking, drinking.

Eldridge said to Cecil, "I want to go home. Give me the keys or I'll take a bus." Cecil didn't want to leave. Tom Luddy asked me for a ride. I said O.K., and he immediately fell into a booth with Ellie Coppola and Jeanette. I told him that he had to come right now. Tom was drunk, happily indifferent to whether he stayed or not. I'd parked around the corner, on Broadway, in front of Adam and Eve, a sex club, and was pleased that my car hadn't been ticketed or towed. Tom sat in the back giving directions to the Bay

Bridge. "Turn right at the corner, turn left at the light. Trust me." I'd made the trip alone ten thousand times, and never once failed to get home. It was confusing to be told to turn right when you intended to turn right.

May 20, '95

Mississippi calls. She says, "All my working life I have done things to help black people. I can drive into the black part of town where no white person would dare to go. I have nothing to fear. They say, 'Hi there, Mizz Mississippi.' I still call them niggers, but only because of the way they act. I'd have an affair with Johnnie Cochran in a minute." Once she said to me, "I don't see why I should have to feel guilty about the Holocaust. It's not my fault." I hadn't been talking or thinking about the Holocaust, and hadn't told anyone to feel guilty. Her remark came out of nowhere. We were in a diner, about to have a sandwich and suddenly the moment was explosive. Simply being a Jew arouses a peculiar expectation mixed with resentment, even in a highly intelligent woman. Amazing to me is that she doesn't do much but watch television, drink beer, and smoke Marlboros, and yet seethes with dark thoughts and tumultuous feeling.

May 22, '95

Wake in the middle of the night coughing. As always, I start to brood and think there is nobody to talk to. Haven't got a friend in the world. It's the middle of the night. Who the hell would I talk to? But I persist in thinking I have no friends and it's always the middle of the night. Then I think maybe I'm a real writer. None of them had anybody to talk to. If they had, none would write. What I mean is too deep for me to understand. Nevertheless, the truth. So back to sleep, conscience clean. My work is done.

June 1, '95

To Britt-Marie's for dinner. Sonny was there with John, whom I'd seen once before, seven years ago, when seeing him had depressed me. The next day Sonny phoned. She asked, "How did John look to you?" I said, "Good." She said, "I'm going to cry." When she asked that question seven years ago, I'd been critical of his jacket and tie, but I wasn't jealous anymore. Jealousy is low and almost universal. I know only two people—Linda Chan and Frank—who simply don't feel it. Once, walking with Sylvia in Greenwich Village, we saw a poster advertising a play that starred a beautiful actress. I said, "Kennedy is screwing her." It was local gossip. Sylvia got mad and said, "You're jealous." Maybe; but more absurd was that she was jealous of my jealousy.

Thousands dedicate their lives to sustaining mass fantasies in politics, news, advertising, public relations, movies, the stock market, etc. An unprecedented dedication to illusions far more powerful than any religious myth.

At Enrico's, a Madonna imitator popped up in front of our table. Loud music begins. Madonna does a dance routine. Hot and acrobatic. Everyone loved it. The pleasure was in knowing she was fake but letting yourself have doubts. It wasn't Madonna, but was it a man or a woman? Why is inauthenticity pleasing, let alone sexy? I thought of evangelical TV preachers. Flashy clothes. Exaggerated emotion. An acted feeling is more effective than a real feeling, since it is magical. Hamlet writes in his daybook: "A man may smile and smile and be a villain." He repeats—"smile and smile." Thus he mocks his struggle to learn this elusive truth. Much harder for me, not half as bright as Hamlet. He doesn't act, though he kills inadvertently or obliquely, not as the direct and immediate result of his intention. He is able to act only as an actor. In the end, he is summoned to his death by Osric, a fop, which is appropriate since neither of them has a natural connection to life.

Ethan goes from place to place with his dog and his computer, his heart and mind.

I went to Stephan's play and had to leave before it ended. He saw me leave. I apologized later; explained that the woman I came with had just returned from Asia, where she'd eaten something that gave her a worm. She felt sick and thought she might throw up. What could be more reasonable and forgiveable? Had she thrown up in the middle of the play, the retching would have ruined the evening for everyone. But Stephan had seen me walk out. In the fixed, deaf look of his eyes, and his little smile of mechanical forgiveness, he forgave nothing. He had the picture of me and Linda in his mind, walking out. Against that picture, nothing reasonable did any good. The more I said the worse it became. I apologized repeatedly, but Stephan had a tremendous moral advantage drawn from pain. He couldn't surrender his pain. He'd invited me to his play. I'd walked out. That was that. His pain was a possession. I'd given it to him, and I couldn't take it away. He is a sweet person with large kind honest eyes and modesty in his voice and gestures. Warm, good, sweet. It kills me to think I gave him pain.

June 21, '95. New York
Black-tie dinner at the Whitney Museum, June 20, to celebrate the opening of the Edward Hopper exhibition. I met Carter Coleman, who'd just returned from Africa, where he'd worked with a conservation group to save a rain forest in the mountains of eastern Tanzania. New York was as hot as Africa. We stood talking in the museum lobby, drinks in hand, sweltering in our tuxedos. There had been a brownout and the air-conditioning failed. Neither of us

mentioned the discomfort. Men and women in fine formal clothes stood all about the lobby. There was a continuous flow of trays bearing delicious finger food and abundant good wine. Then came the sudden, hot, dense feeling of the air. Carter stopped telling me about the rain forest and gestured vaguely with his drink, as if to include everything—the sumptuousness of our surroundings, the whole lovely occasion. I think what he wanted to say—but couldn't say this moment—was apparent, and related to the rain forest in Tanzania.

At dinner, I was seated beside a woman named Nan, who looked at the bowl of flowers in the center of the table and said it was obviously expensive. She wished the people who organized the occasion would sell it and give the money to the museum. She asked who I was. I told her I'd written about Hopper for the catalogue. She said, "Well, I'm a donor. We're important, too." I said, "You're indispensable," and asked if she was in business. She said, "I own a little oil company." I asked if she goes to an office. "Not every day," she said, "but often enough." She'd find it unbearable to stay home always and "listen to the vacuum cleaner in the next apartment." She talked about dinners she remembered in her childhood. "I'm seventy," she said. "In those days women went to a certain room after dinner, and the men went to another where they smoked cigars and talked about business." She said she'd follow her father and the other men, and make herself very small so they wouldn't see her. She would listen to their talk. "I loved it very much," she said, and she showed me how she scrunched up, imitating herself as a little girl in a room full of men and cigars and business talk.

June 23, '95. New York
The Lower East Side was a tough neighborhood, mafia-controlled, but I wasn't afraid to come home at any hour and walk the five or

six blocks from the subway to our apartment building. It was safe. Our gangsters had family values. But the gangsters have moved to Long Island. Mikey, Jerry, Manny, Tony, Louie, Frankie, Carmelo, Buffalo—why did you leave? At night I have to take a taxi to my mother's building. Inside the building, I ride the elevator to the fourteenth floor, still uneasy. I walk down the hall fingering three keys, and then turn them quietly in the locks. I don't want to wake my mother. There used to be one lock, one key. Opening a door was simple, no challenge to your dignity. I can't immediately remember which key is for which lock. Tumblers rattle and my mother springs out of bed, her little naked feet thumping to the door. "Who is it? Who is it?" she cries. I say, "It's me." The hall is resonant with the sound of elevators. They are whining in the black hollow shaft, an ominous *nnnnn* from the throat of the building. Hurry, open the door. It opens. My mother goes back to sleep. I'm still too vigilant. I go to the window. I can see uptown, all the way to the Chrysler Building. The infinite city is ablaze. Ambulances and police cars are screaming along Delancey Street, streaking the night.

June 25, '95
Driving back to Berkeley after the anthropology conference with Lenora Johanson. Traffic was heavy and slow. I felt the bridge swaying high above the bay. Lenora said she keeps a wet suit in the trunk of her car. If there were an earthquake and the bridge collapsed, she could put on the wet suit and swim home. I imagined the long fall to the bay. I had no wet suit. Besides, I can hardly swim.

Sonny went to the doctor and met Horace in the waiting room. She hadn't seen him in years. When she said, "Horace," he looked toward her, not at her, and there was no recognition in his eyes. She then realized he couldn't see, he was blind. She identified herself. He reached toward her with open arms. They embraced. She offered him a ride home. He was delighted. Then Sonny had to hang around waiting for his examination to end, but it took only a half hour. She drove him home. He invited her in for tea. She thought his house is cleaner than hers, but of course he must have a maid. She offered to help with the tea, but he wouldn't let her do anything, so she had to watch him fumble with the cups and saucers, though he did everything else smoothly. He said, "I remember that you're beautiful."

"You can't see that I've aged."

"I can't."

"That's wonderful," said Sonny, laughing, entirely confident that Horace would be amused by her response, not offended or hurt. Sonny takes these little liberties and people find her charming because she means no harm and she is beautiful. Horace didn't laugh. He wasn't offended or hurt, but his blindness wasn't amusing to him. Nor did it make him grim. He talked about it to Sonny, telling her how it began with little things. He'd knock over a salt shaker or a glass of wine. While driving he'd almost hit people or drive blithely through a red light. His doctor thought Horace was under extraordinary stress and his blindness was psychological. Finally, Horace went to an ophthalmologist who discovered that, from an angle, Horace couldn't see anything. The ophthalmologist diagnosed Horace's blindness as congenital. Sonny asked if Horace could hear better since becoming blind. Horace said no, and assured Sonny that compensatory improvement in hearing is a myth. He offered to make her a sandwich. In fact, Sonny was a little hungry, but she said no thanks because she didn't want to watch him fumbling about in the kitchen. She said his eyes were teary, as if with love. She thought perhaps he was remembering what she looked like years ago. She'd been loved for her looks ever since she was a little girl, and men continued to love her for her looks even now in her forties, but she'd never been loved by a blind man. It brought tears to her eyes, too, Horace's memory of her. His memory was all he could see, so it was as if they were both young, and he was overcome by her beauty.

It's been said that when you sleep the soul floats free of the body and takes a look at things not otherwise available for contemplation. If the soul looks into the future, prophetic dreams must come. Other souls would prefer to look into the past. To float free of the body, after all, is to float free of time, and it must then be equally possible to look ahead or back.

Personally, I'm more interested in the past than in visions of the future, which is, I'm afraid, ultimately the same for all of us. The past, however, is full of mystery of the most personal kind. Indeed, it might be the only thing we have that is personal. Reading my journal, hearing my voice of long ago, I felt disembodied, and rather ghostly, as I contemplated the man back there in the midst of life, from his twenties onward. There is mystery in what he thought, and what happened to him from one year to the next, at least as far as I'm concerned. I seem almost to contemplate a stranger. He did and said things I'd never do, never say. I want to claim he isn't me. Anyhow, not entirely me. But the journal is in my voice. All the notebooks are in my handwriting. Given such evidence, I have no choice but to conclude that I am, in a very personal sense, that man. And yet a doubt remains. Can it be that we are merely ourselves? Montaigne, contemplating the picture of himself created in his book of essays, says his book made him as much as he made his book. This leads him to a curious intuition. Montaigne feels more unlike himself than he is unlike others. I sympathize with all my heart.